LASTING IMPRESSIONS

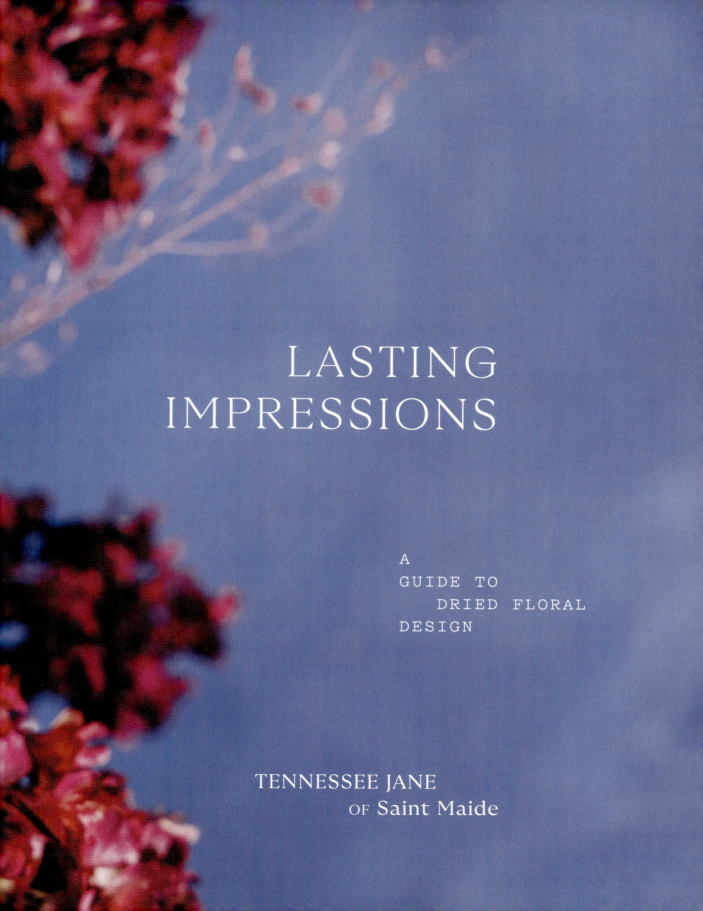

LASTING IMPRESSIONS

A
GUIDE TO
DRIED FLORAL
DESIGN

TENNESSEE JANE
OF Saint Maide

Library of Congress Cataloging-in-Publication Data is on file.

ISBN 978-1-64829-404-4

Photographs by Kate Dearman and Kylie Hull
Design by Nina Simoneaux

Artisan books may be purchased in bulk for business, educational, or promotional use. For information, please contact your local bookseller or the Hachette Book Group Special Markets Department at special.markets@hbgusa.com.

The publisher is not responsible for websites (or their content) that are not owned by the publisher.

The Hachette Speakers Bureau provides a wide range of authors for speaking events. To find out more, go to hachettespeakersbureau.com or email HachetteSpeakers@hbgusa.com.

Published by Artisan,
an imprint of Workman Publishing,
a division of Hachette Book Group, Inc.
1290 Avenue of the Americas
New York, NY 10104
artisanbooks.com

The Artisan name and logo are registered trademarks of Hachette Book Group, Inc.

Printed in China (TLF) on responsibly sourced paper

First printing, July 2025

10 9 8 7 6 5 4 3 2 1

To all the burned-out millennials

CONTENTS

Introduction

As a floral designer, I never expected what became some of my favorite feedback: "This reminds me of something that my mom had in our house as a kid," or "This is just like a bouquet I was once gifted and kept past its expiration date." Dried flowers leave a lasting impression on us, as they are often closely tied to a deeply personal, sentimental memory. Call it the millennial obsession with nostalgia, but one of the reasons I love dried florals is that they come with a story—a previous life—and as a designer of dried floral arrangements, I get to unpack those histories each time I make one.

When I started my dried floral design studio, Saint Maide, I chose the word *evocative* to describe the type of work I was going to create. It means "bringing strong images, memories, or feelings to mind," and the arrangements I design are intended to do just that. It may be a cheery sentiment, a bittersweet memory, or an overwhelming sense of peace, but the tie between florals and feeling is undeniable. And you'll see this connection reflected in the chapters that follow: the bright, statement-making pieces in "Bold"; minimal, earthy projects in "Calm"; colorful, celebratory designs in "Joyful"; romantic, feminine arrangements in "Wistful"; and eye-catching modern holiday décor in "Festive."

The other word I often use to describe my work is *elevated*. We may have some outdated notions of dried florals from decades past; I design with the intention to elevate the arrangements beyond these expectations. Dried florals have so much potential, and their untapped versatility is finally being recognized by floral enthusiasts and designers alike.

Helping you tap into *your* artistic potential and express it through dried florals is the true goal of this book. To that end, the Getting Started section covers everything you need to know to begin working with dried florals, including how to source, dry, and even store your materials. Then I'll walk you step-by-step through the creation of 52 dried floral designs, from tabletop arrangements to hand-tied bouquets, wall hangings to small-scale floral installations. The Library of Ingredients is a survey of some of my favorite plant matter and how best to dry and arrange it, and Resources includes my go-to destinations for dried plant material, tools, and more. Soon enough, you'll be creating your very own evocative and elevated dried floral designs.

Getting Started

When I first embarked on my dried floral journey, there weren't a ton of up-to-date resources at my disposal, and I made a lot of assumptions based on what I knew about working with fresh-cut flowers. While there is some overlap between the two—such as the use of support structures, and many of the design techniques—I've learned a lot as I've continued to work with dried materials.

The following pages include everything you need to know to complete the designs in this book, plus some key information and context I wish someone had taught me when I was first experimenting with dried florals. From how to process, prepare, and properly store them to basic wreath- and bouquet-making techniques, and even how to dry your own flowers, you'll be armed with the intel you need to confidently complete your dried floral designs.

Types of Dried Florals

There are a few different terms you'll come across when you venture into the world of dried florals. The floral industry lumps any dried material (flowers, grasses, branches, pods, and more) under the term *dried florals*, and I often do so as well, but there *are* distinctions to be aware of, as some types involve chemically altering the plants to preserve them. Here's a quick primer.

Dried. Preserved plant life, including flowers, grasses, branches, and pods, resulting in textured, brittle stems that are beautiful in their own right. The moisture has been removed from the material through a drying process, without application of other substances, as seen here with the dried mini foxtail millet grass. (For a tutorial on drying your own florals, see page 32.)

Preserved. Stems that have been treated to remain flexible and retain movement, like the leather fern pictured here. Amaranthus and eucalyptus, for example, are often sold in their preserved state. If you are purchasing preserved stems from a commercial wholesaler or outlet, chemicals were likely used to treat the material.

Bleached. Bleach is used to both preserve the plant material and alter its color, making it appear bright white. Ruscus and baby's breath are two commonly found bleached materials; the less common craspedia is pictured here. (Note that bleached stems often yellow over time.)

These days, most of us want to prioritize sustainability. This often starts with where you shop, what materials you source, and how they have been treated prior to purchase. Always ask for more information from sellers about how they're using these terms if you're in doubt!

FROM TOP TO BOTTOM: Preserved leather fern, dried mini foxtail millet grass, and bleached craspedia

Sourcing

There are so many outlets from which to source dried florals that it may feel overwhelming. Big-box craft stores will likely carry the most common dried flowers. I also recommend seeking out local flower farms, which may carry a selection of dried stems in the fall and winter months. You can buy many types of dried ingredients online these days—see page 216 for some of my go-to resources. (Whenever trying a new supplier, I recommend buying a small amount at first, because quality can vary widely.) Of course, you might also opt to purchase fresh stems to dry yourself—see pages 32–33 for some basic techniques.

A note on foraging: To err on the side of caution, only take plant life that has naturally fallen or broken off. Otherwise, always ask permission from the owner of the land you're on.

SUSTAINABILITY

To make the most informed and sustainable purchasing decisions, you'll want to know the provenance of your materials.

The assumption that dried florals are always more sustainable than fresh-cut ingredients is a fallacy. There are multiple factors to consider when thinking about the environmental impact of our material choices, including the carbon footprint of transport, whether a chemical preservation treatment was used, if you will be employing any additional treatments such as aerosol paint to color them, and what you will use to support them.

I like to look at sustainability on a spectrum, especially when it comes to using dried materials. If you're a staunch naturalist, you will likely want to avoid anything preserved or bleached, work with all local ingredients, and avoid any nonreusable support structures. If you're hoping to play around with color-treated materials—or you're a floral designer whose client wants a particular look—you may have to make some compromises; you might consider

> ### A NOTE ON PLANT NAMES AND QUANTITIES
>
> I have used the common names of flowers for all the projects in this book. The Library of Ingredients, beginning on page 204, includes scientific names and other common names for each plant. When it comes to quantities, there are no set standards for the number of stems in a bunch, so I have listed most ingredient quantities as a number of stems (except in the cases of dried grasses and tree branches). For any given project, you'll want to have a few more stems on hand than the listed number, however, as dried florals are finicky and brittle, and you will undoubtedly lose some along the way.

coloring your florals yourself (see page 34 for a basic tutorial) or opt for a reusable support system such as chicken wire to prioritize sustainability in other aspects of the design.

There will be many decisions during the design process, from material selection to finishing touches, that will give you the opportunity to make the more sustainable choice. I encourage you to explore your options and prioritize sustainability whenever possible.

Tools

These are the tools of the trade. All can be found online or in hardware and craft stores, and you don't need the most expensive or fanciest option to get the job done well. If you're a floral enthusiast or crafter, you'll likely already have a number of these on hand.

1. **Kitchen scissors.** A low-cost alternative to fancy floral snips, these handle brittle stems with ease.

2. **Chicken wire.** My most frequently used support structure. It's available in large rolls, but a little goes a long way. The coated variety is superior as it's easier on the hands.

3. **Zip ties.** The secret workhorse in most florists' toolboxes, zip ties make complicated mechanics a breeze. They're frequently used to secure bundles of dried material and for creating large-scale installations.

4. **Hot glue gun.** The tool I often reach for to secure delicate floral bits. It will come in handy time and time again, especially for wreaths and long-term installations.

5. **Rocks.** Due to the lightweight nature of dried materials, I frequently reach for inexpensive landscaping rocks to help weight down vessels, eliminating the worry of an arrangement toppling over.

6. **Fishing line.** This comes in handy for hanging installations. Using a smaller line diameter (0.010 inch or 10.1 pound/0.25 mm) will minimize the appearance of the mechanics. Choose the appropriate size for the weight of the arrangement you are hanging, as each diameter can only accommodate a certain weight.

7. **Pin frog.** Also called a kenzan and frequently referred to as a flower frog, this is the traditional foundation for ikebana-style arrangements. Available in various shapes and sizes, this must-have tool can be reused over and over to create designs in various styles.

8. **Floral tape.** There are multiple kinds of floral tape on the market, but the two I use most frequently are clear cellophane tape and floral stem wrap tape. Both are water resistant, but the floral stem wrap tape has adhesive that is activated when the tape is stretched. Clear tape is great for creating grid supports on vessels, and it is especially useful when crafting light and airy floral arrangements. Floral stem wrap tape is best for bundling stems or securing a bouquet.

9. **Toothpicks.** Perfect for securing bulky or oddly shaped flower heads in sculptural arrangements.

10. **Hairpin frog.** A favorite support structure for sculptural arrangements, a hairpin frog is a type of flower frog especially great for securing thin, delicate dried stems.

11. **Bind wire.** Frequently used for wreaths, this paper-coated wire comes in botanical brown and green shades and is easily concealed.

12. **Floral putty.** A nondamaging adhesive, used to secure flower frogs in vessels.

13. **Paddle wire.** This easy-to-handle floral wire, available in different gauges, is wrapped flat, making it ideal for wreath making.

14. **Twine.** A low-cost material for securing bouquets or bundling ingredients for storage.

15. **Floral shears, pruners, and snips.** Each is an absolute necessity, available in different sizes. Pruners, shown here, can easily deal with the tough stems that often come with the territory of dried materials.

Floral pins (not pictured). Also known as greening pins, these U-shaped steel fasteners help secure moss, greenery and other small flower parts to wreaths and topiaries. They're reusable, so be sure to hold on to them after each use.

Vases and Other Vessels

One of the upsides to working with dried florals is that you never need to worry about keeping an arrangement hydrated. This means you can use nontraditional vessels, as they do not have to hold water. One thing to keep in mind: The size of the vessel's opening will determine the overall size of the arrangement. Since dried florals have lost a lot of their volume during the drying process, a widemouthed container will necessitate a lot more dried materials than a similarly sized arrangement of fresh blooms. And whatever vessel you choose, remember to keep landscaping rocks handy, as you may need extra weight in the bottom of the vessel to keep your dried arrangement from toppling over.

Here are a few tried-and-true shapes that I find myself returning to again and again for their versatility and aesthetic appeal.

Pedestal vase/compote. These footed vessels tend to be showstoppers and make great centerpieces.

Bouquet vase. In this common shape, the opening gently flares out, giving a little more space to tightly packed bouquet stems and creating a sense of movement in the overall arrangement.

Tall, narrow vase. This vertical-style shape is ideal for showcasing a few statement stems or feathery grasses.

Widemouthed vase. Also commonly referred to as a bowl vase, this type of vessel is well suited to dense floral arrangements.

Bud vase. These miniature vases are perfect for displaying a few standout dried stems. If using multiples in a group, choose vases of varying heights to add visual interest.

Round vase. These are ideal for short, sculptural arrangements.

Low bowl/dish. You'll need to use a flower frog (see page 14) with these vessels, which are frequently used for ikebana-inspired designs.

Jug. Two-handled vessels with narrower necks and rounded bodies, also called amphora vases, are based on ancient Greek and Roman designs that were used primarily for transporting liquids.

Unconventional vessels. Keep your eyes peeled at vintage markets and antique fairs for anything that can be used as a vessel—you don't have to worry about it holding water, so look for nontraditional, unique pieces like sculptural bronze works or even candleholders to create one-of-kind floral designs. Pictured here is a teacup, but I've also used shot glasses, cinder blocks, plastic tubing, shells, and test tubes. As long as you can attach your stems, there are no limits to what you can use!

Preparing Your Dried Ingredients

Taking the time and care to do these important first steps will not only help you re-create the arrangements in this book but will also give you an advantage when it comes time to create your own dried floral designs.

PROCESSING

Whether you're purchasing dried flowers online or from a wholesaler or retail store, they will almost always arrive in need of processing. In floral design, this term refers to the readying of stems for arranging. In fresh floral design this includes removing leaves and thorns, cutting stems, and preparing the stems for placement in water. Since we don't have to worry about water, and because the stems have dried to an inflexible state, processing dried flowers is a little more straightforward.

Unless otherwise stated, all arrangements in this book utilize processed stems, free of dead leaves and dry greenery. Since dried stems are brittle, take care to remove the leaves one by one so as not to break the stem. I recommend wearing gloves when removing leaves from dried materials as they can be sharp and thorns are often still intact.

Since we are not rushing to get stems into water as with fresh florals, stem cutting is less critical to the success of your finished arrangement. However, as the last step in processing my materials, I always like to give a very slight trim to the ends prior to design, for consistency's sake. I recommend leaving the stems long until you are ready to design and know exactly what length(s) will be needed.

I tend to process stems as soon as I receive them, even if I don't yet have a design in mind. If you're not able to process stems before storing them, I recommend at least removing the rubber band that often comes on commercial bundles, as it tends to flatten out the stems.

BUNDLING

This simple preparation is extremely helpful when you're trying to achieve more density and/or maximum color impact with a dried ingredient. The number of stems needed will ultimately depend on the size of your arrangement, but I recommend bundling a few together and testing them out in your piece before committing to a size.

   Note: If you are grouping a one-sided ingredient, as shown above, take care to face the heads of the florals in the same direction so that a look of abundant color is achieved. You can use rubber bands to group stems together, but I prefer floral tape for one-sided stems so they will not move once bundled.

STORING

Properly wrapping and storing your fragile materials is key to maximizing their shelf life and keeping them in tip-top shape. After you've processed and bundled your dried florals and stems, wrap them with either tissue paper (for delicate blooms like ranunculus and paper daisies) or kraft paper (for heartier stems like strawflowers). This will prevent them from tangling, which at best is frustrating and at worst results in broken stems and decapitated flower heads.

   After you've wrapped the bundles, you can store them upright in a bucket; keep them away from direct sunlight. Heat and light speed up the aging process, so a cool, dark room is best. If you won't be using your materials soon, pack them in shallow, weatherproof boxes away from any critters that might want to take up residence in them.

Foundational Support Structures

I often refer to the support system of an arrangement as its *mechanics*, a term that encompasses all the devices and methods used to secure materials and create stability in an arrangement. It is the foundation of all of your floral work. The following mechanics are tried and true—they're surprisingly simple to incorporate into your floral designs, and most are reusable.

CHICKEN WIRE

This sustainable option works in most vessels. Simply ball and scrunch up a section of chicken wire and stick it in your vessel to provide stability for stems. The more chicken wire you use and the more densely you roll it, the denser the arrangement can be. Use a bit less for a lighter, airy design. Chicken wire can also add support for heavy wreaths and larger installations.

TAPE GRID

Hands down the easiest support method. Simply use floral tape to create a grid across the top of any vessel. As you add stems, the grid will be hidden. Colored floral tape is best for lush, full designs; clear tape is less adhesive but preferable for airier arrangements where you don't want the grid to distract from the final design. You can employ asymmetrical grids to create free-flowing and more whimsical arrangements.

FLOWER FROG

This is one of the most frequently used support structures for floral designers. Use floral putty to secure a flower frog (pin or hairpin type) inside the vessel, pushing down to strengthen the bond between the frog and the vessel. I like to layer chicken wire on top of flower frogs followed by a tape grid for additional support, especially when using heavy branches or ingredients that need a strong foundation to stay upright.

ZIP TIES

I most often use zip ties for installations and hanging arrangements, but they can also be used in a pinch to bundle heavy-duty stems and larger bundles of materials. Once you've created the preferred shape with your materials or identified where an arrangement needs additional support, simply pass the pointy end of the zip tie through the self-locking top and pull it through to secure it. (I find the clicking sound immensely satisfying.) Don't forget to trim the excess end of the zip tie so there are no distracting plastic pieces hanging off.

A good example of all these design principles working in harmony is this airy arrangement featuring golden and cottage yarrow, cress, and craspedia. Notice how the use of negative space helps impart a sense of lightness to the design.

Design Principles

Traditionally, dried floral designs centered around dense arrangements made with very vertical, brightly colored filler flowers and secondary stems, since these types of flowers dry easily. But as design sensibilities have shifted, so too have ways of working and designing with dried florals—as you'll see in the projects that follow.

Sometimes I'll use a single ingredient to make a sculptural arrangement, use typically overlooked stems as the focal flower, or add unexpected pieces to produce a sense of movement. These arrangements are meant to serve as art and décor, after all, so I like to seek inspiration from other art forms like sculpture, painting, and especially interior design to boost my creativity.

There are no hard-and-fast rules to follow, especially with dried flowers, but here are five principles of floral design that will undoubtedly help you understand what makes for a successful composition.

FORM

In this book, I often instruct you to create an arrangement in a certain shape, like a triangle—this is the design's form. I also refer to *anchor stems*; these are the pieces I'll build my arrangement or bouquet around to determine its overall form. Form can also refer to the shape of the individual ingredients, such as straight vertical stems, round flower heads, or curved branches.

PROPORTION

Proportion refers to the relationship of individual elements to one another as well as to the arrangement as a whole. It can also be discussed in terms of the size of the arrangement to the vessel (a good rule to follow for the arrangement-to-vessel height ratio is 2:1). This is undoubtedly one of the tougher design principles to wrap your head around, because the materials we are working with are three-dimensional. You can think about it this way: All of the elements in an arrangement—the flowers, foliage, vessel, and their respective shapes and colors—are in conversation. If they're on good terms, the design will feel at peace. If they're not, the arrangement will seem off-kilter.

Don't shy away from varying the sizes and proportions of your materials; playing around with individual ingredients (for instance, placing one oversized flower head alongside soft grasses in a tabletop installation or using a single uniform element in an asymmetrically shaped arrangement) can push the boundaries of your design skills and lead to successful, unexpected outcomes. Experimenting with the principles of proportion will help you discover what style of floral design you like and help you become a stronger designer in the process.

SCALE

Closely related to proportion is scale, the size of the piece relative to its setting. Since many dried arrangements are intended as interior décor, this is an important element to consider from the very beginning of the process. Designing with the dimensions of the intended space in mind will produce an arrangement that looks right at home.

SPACE

Consider the open areas around the individual components. Many designers use the term *negative space* to refer to this unoccupied space in an arrangement. Traditional dried floral designs tend to have very little negative space, resulting in a dense, lush look. If you prefer a light and airy aesthetic, you will want to allow for more negative space in your designs.

COLOR

Since color preferences are subjective, there is no exact formula for choosing a color palette. But the basics of color theory can be used to inform our choices and produce pleasing harmonies in a design. Here are a few ways I approach creating color palettes for my floral designs, using the color wheel:

Monochromatic: Different hues of a single color (e.g., pink, red, and maroon)

Analogous: Three or more colors that sit next to one another on the color wheel (e.g., yellow, yellow-orange, and orange)

Complementary: A combination of hues that sit opposite each other on the color wheel (e.g., yellow and purple)

Triad: Three colors that are equally spaced on the color wheel (e.g., red, blue, and yellow)

The result of all of these elements working together is what can be termed *visual interest*. I first heard designer Athena Calderone use this phrase, meaning that "it engages the eye, allowing it to dance from one [element] to the next"; it perfectly encapsulates that quality I often try to create when I design dried floral arrangements. Your eye should be compelled to keep moving throughout the design, resulting in an arrangement that feels both evocative and elevated.

CARING FOR DRIED ARRANGEMENTS

I often get asked how long dried florals will last and how best to care for them so they will stay in first-rate condition. In my experience, they can hold up well for years, though they will likely fade a bit over time. Keeping them out of direct sunlight will help slow this process. Use a feather duster to gently clean the arrangements, as it won't break delicate leaves or stems. Finally, keep them away from pets, as some ingredients can be toxic for animals.

How to Build a Wreath

Creating wreaths can be intimidating, especially to a beginner, but here are a few foundational techniques that will quickly help you master these designs in no time.

CHOOSING YOUR BASE

A critical determining factor of the overall look and feel of a wreath is the type of base you choose to use. The thickness of the wreath base will determine the fullness and amount of material you need for your design, so decide on the base before you buy any floral materials. A straw base will produce a denser wreath, as will a metal wreath form. For a lighter, airy design, I recommend using a skinny grapevine base or a decorative single wreath ring.

A number of premade options are available on the market (such as the straw base pictured opposite, top), which will speed up the design process. Alternatively, you can create your own grapevine base (pictured opposite, bottom) using a roll of vine (available at many craft stores) or foraging for wild grapevine. Just cut the vine a little longer than your desired circumference, overlap the two ends, and tightly tie them off with sturdy floral or bind wire to ensure it stays connected.

PREPARING YOUR BASE

No matter what option you choose for your base, whether premade or handmade, you'll likely need to wrap it with either chicken wire or bind wire so that the floral stems, pieces, and any other materials stay in place. Wrapping with chicken wire will ensure that heavier materials are adequately supported, while wrapping with bind wire is better for more delicate designs.

Depending on the design, wrap either the entire base or just the section that will have florals attached. When using chicken wire, I recommend using just enough to allow stems to pass through but not so much that it looks baggy sitting on the base. Use a zip tie to secure it to the back of the base. If you are using bind wire, tightly wrap the base in a crisscross pattern and tie it off on the back; this will ensure delicate stems have a snug place to sit. You won't need to fill in with additional materials to cover it because bind wire is easily camouflaged in natural-colored bases such as grapevine.

BUNDLING AND BUILDING

I've found that thinking about wreaths as parts that combine into a whole is a good way to approach building them—it's easier to focus on completing the small steps, and before you know it you'll have a finished product. To that end, here's a method I've dubbed the *bundle and build* technique. It's quite simple to master, and with a few tries, you'll be able to confidently make the lush wreaths that this technique produces.

Start by creating small bundles of your chosen ingredients, ensuring the most aesthetically pleasing part of the stem faces up and outward. Vary the placement of the individual flower heads in each bundle to create a sense of movement throughout the wreath. The width of each bundle and the total number of bundles needed will depend on the size of your wreath base. Keep extra stems on hand to fill in anywhere that looks sparse after you've secured the bundles.

Next, map out your design by layering the bundles so that they slightly overlap one another in a ring to determine the best order and placement.

Once you have figured out where each bundle will go, insert the first one in the wreath and tightly secure it with paddle wire.

Repeat this step, layering the bundles to cover the stems and creating a lush, full wreath. The last bundle you'll insert will be the trickiest, as you need to attach it so that it doesn't stick out; it should be flush with the rest of the wreath. You can simply tuck the final bundle into the others, but I recommend weaving wire delicately in between stems and tying it off on the back to keep it in place. If needed, fill in any gaps or holes with the extra loose stems that you saved in the beginning.

1

4

2

3

5

6

How to Create a Hand-Tied Bouquet

All of the bouquets featured in this book are hand tied, which is a simple and accessible approach for designers of all skill levels. This method may tire your hand a bit, but it is ultimately foolproof. The bouquets you create are unlikely to have *all* of the elements discussed here, but this strategy and technique will help you to re-create the projects in this book as well as design your own.

CREATING YOUR FRAMEWORK

Hold three of the sturdiest vertical stems so their heads form an open triangle. I like to incorporate at least one stem that has a slight bend or curve to give a sense of movement. These will form the shape and height of the bouquet and act as anchor stems. Be sure the bottoms of the stems cross over one another, which will create a support structure for the others you'll add in. The tricky part will be to hold these materials loosely enough that you can place additional stems but tightly enough that the shape holds.

FILLING IN YOUR BOUQUET

Add filler or denser flowers between your vertical stems in a crisscross fashion. Next, add your focal flowers. I like to employ these in multiples of three or another odd number to keep the eye moving when you look at the finished arrangement. Fill in any holes or anywhere you want to feel lusher with additional secondary (denser) flowers. If you want to make a larger bouquet, continue adding both focal and secondary stems one at a time, taking care to keep the balance and weight of the arrangement even.

TRIMMING THE ENDS

Once you've placed all your materials in the bouquet, hold the bouquet tightly with one hand and use the other to trim the stems to an even length.

TYING IT OFF

Finish by tying off the bouquet with twine or ribbon. It is slightly easier to lay it flat and tie it, but I find the bouquet will hold its shape better if you do it one-handed. Or better yet, ask someone to help you tie it off!

Drying Your Own Florals

Since I am by no means a professional gardener or grower with a full-scale drying operation, I've been motivated to find the easiest at-home methods that produce the most professional results. Here are the techniques I have found to be most successful. In the Library of Ingredients (page 204), you can see my go-to drying methods for specific florals.

AIR-DRYING

The easiest technique by far, this is your "set it and forget it" method. Simply process your stems to avoid tangling, put them in a container—a vase or even a bucket—where the flower heads have enough room to breathe, and leave them for a few weeks without water in a low-humidity room. This method is ideal for stems like statice and limonium that need little to no care while drying; it also works for more delicate stems like scabiosa pods that need extra room during the drying process. This allows the stems to dry with a slight bend or curve, as they will lean out and over the side of the container.

EVAPORATION

If you've ever left a fresh bouquet in a vase and come back to find it perfectly dried, you have unknowingly used the evaporation method. Also referred to as vase drying, it's just what the name implies: Put your stems in a vase with a small amount of water and leave them to slowly dry out over the course of days or weeks, ensuring that a *small* amount of water remains in the vase throughout the drying process. I like to leave no more than ½ inch (1.3 cm) of water in the vase to avoid any potential mold growth. Check on your stems every other day to ensure they have enough water. As they dry out, you'll notice they drink less and less water, and the flower heads should start to look crisp. Once they're fully dried, you'll need to process the ends of the stems that were submerged. You may be able to just wipe them off; if they're moldy, trim and discard the expired bits. This method is best suited for stems with cluster heads, such as hydrangea, ammi, and baby's breath.

HANG-DRYING

This method is one you've no doubt seen in books and on flower farms: loads of bundled flowers hanging from the ceiling, creating a canopy of color. It's a gorgeous effect—and you can use this method even if you have just a bundle or two of flowers to dry. Since I have a relatively small workspace and dry only a few bundles at a time, I like to hang them from a ladder instead of the ceiling.

Process and bundle your florals, hang them upside down, and leave them for a few weeks, until they've dried.

This method works for most varieties. It is especially great for ensuring flowers keep their color, as the last remaining moisture will settle down into the flower heads, helping to preserve their vibrancy.

MICROWAVING

The microwave is best suited for drying small flower heads and petals. Have I used this method in a pinch? Yes. Do I recommend it? Mostly no. While commercial operations dehydrate florals by machine, it is difficult to replicate their results at home. That being said, here is what I advise if you want to try using the microwave to dry flowers; I highly recommend you test this method with a few stems before doing a large batch, as microwaves can vary. Layer your pieces between damp paper towels and microwave them for two minutes on 50 percent power. Check on the florals and continue microwaving them in fifteen-second intervals until they reach your desired dryness and texture.

OVEN-DRYING

While I have experimented with drying florals in the oven, it has never produced results I was happy with. However, when it comes to drying fruit for festive arrangements, I absolutely recommend the oven. Slice fruit ½ inch (1.3 cm) thick, lay the slices flat on a parchment paper–covered sheet pan, and bake at 225°F (110°C) for approximately eight hours, turning them over a few times to prevent the rind from darkening. Cool completely on a wire rack, then store in resealable bags or containers and check periodically to ensure there are no pieces with any remaining moisture (if so, discard them to prevent the growth of mildew/mold).

Coloring Your Own Florals

You'll see painted pieces called for in some of the arrangements in this book. If you've never painted dried florals, do not be intimidated! Although these methods are more labor intensive than simply purchasing precolored stems, they allow you to develop color to your exact specifications—a nice option to have as a designer. Here are a few tried-and-true methods for coloring your own florals, which produce distinct but equally stunning finishes.

SPRAY-PAINTING

This is my most-used technique for painting dried florals. The dehydrated stems and petals readily absorb paint, making for maximum color payoff.

There are many types of spray paint on the market, from epoxy to acrylic to lacquer, but I use only two types on dried florals. The first is floral spray paint, a modified lacquer paint that has been created specifically for use on fresh floral stems. It is a semi-transparent paint, imparting a wash of color for a subtle effect. The second is acrylic spray paint, which you will find in art stores. It imparts an opaque layer of color. It's colorfast and easy to use, great for creating bright, bold designs. This is the type of spray paint that I most often reach for, and unless otherwise noted, it is the type used for the arrangements in this book.

Be sure to wear a face mask when using spray paint—otherwise it's nearly impossible to avoid breathing it in—and always work in a well-ventilated area, ideally outside. Lay down paper to avoid painting a surface that you didn't intend to, and place your materials on it. When using any type of spray paint, shake the can vigorously, as this will help distribute the color particles throughout the liquid. Start slowly: Do one even coat first and see how you like it. If you want more color, you can always do multiple coats. Let the materials dry between coats.

When you paint waxy material such as palm fronds, the paint tends to bead off, but with multiple coats you'll achieve the look you're after. No matter what material you paint, let it dry thoroughly before using it in an arrangement.

DYEING

If spray paint is not your thing, or you're looking for a more sustainable option, dye is a great alternative. This method works best on heartier stems that have fluffy or fuzzy flower heads, such as bunny tails and pampas grass; the dye solution imparts a beautiful, muted tone.

I recommend doing small batches of stems so you'll be able to keep a closer eye on how the process is unfolding. Add food coloring to a small amount of water. The intensity of the color will depend on how much dye you add and how many stems you are processing. Dip the dried flower heads facedown into the solution, with the stems resting against the side of the jar. Leave them submerged until you start to see the color penetrating the flower heads—this will likely take a couple of hours. Once you've achieved the desired color, remove the stems, blot them with paper towels, and hang- or air-dry them (see pages 32–33).

BLEACHING

I recommend buying bleached products from commercial sources rather than trying this yourself—in my experience, bleaching materials at home can result in yellowish stems, not the crisp white look you're likely after. However, in a pinch I have used a very watered-down bleach solution (1 part bleach to 20 parts water) to lighten fluffy stems like pampas. If you go this route, instead of soaking the stems, put the solution in a spray bottle and apply it in a very well-ventilated area. Spray a few coats, wait for them to dry, and assess the result. Do a second round if necessary; I wouldn't suggest doing more than that, as the stem will likely yellow.

Alternatively, you can leave stems outside to be bleached naturally by the sun. It is not a quick process (it will take weeks), nor will it give you a bright white result, but it is the most environmentally friendly option and yields an equally beautiful stem.

BOLD

I.

Looking for dried florals that will stop you in your tracks? Look no further. These colorful, eye-catching designs will have you asking *Is this art?* (To which I say, *Yes, we are artists, and dried florals are our medium!*) Though I don't normally gravitate toward bold florals, designing these arrangements pushed me out of my comfort zone and brought a lot more color into my life; they quickly became some of my favorite pieces I've ever designed. From a Schiaparelli-inspired entryway arrangement to a suspended hanging branch, in this chapter we'll experiment with funky forms and unexpected color schemes to create evocative, unusual dried floral arrangements that reflect our bolder inclinations.

Curvy Tsunami Palm Fronds

What You'll Need

Large round narrow-neck
  vase
Chicken wire
3 tsunami palm fronds
3 stems oleander seed
  pods
3 stems inula
3 stems preserved
  dark green hanging
  amaranthus
2 curly willow branches

Before I became a floral designer, I worked in fashion, and among the things I loved most about witnessing the design process were the inspiration boards that were created for each collection. Gathering design references from across the decades—sourcing from the fine arts, decorative arts and crafts, and interior design, to name just a few influences—and seeing how those references were interpreted and served as inspiration were among my biggest lessons from the fashion industry. Anything can be the seed of an idea for your next creation.

In the case of this arrangement, my inspiration was Elsa Schiaparelli, an Italian fashion designer known for her bold, oftentimes sculptural designs. Sourcing tsunami palm fronds will be critical to the success of this arrangement as you really want to be able to play with their bold shapes. A wholesaler is your best bet; since they often sell only to design professionals, check with a local florist to see if they can source them for you.

1. Insert a small amount of chicken wire into the vase for stability.

2. Place a palm frond in the center back, angled upward. (Note that since the fronds are top-heavy, they will move around as you add more stems to the arrangement.)

3. Add a second palm frond on the right so its inside faces downward and is flush with the vase.

4. Trim the oleander seed pods and place them in the center of the arrangement to create a more stable structure for the remaining stems.

5. Trim the inula and add them shooting out from just behind the oleander.

6. Drape the amaranthus over and along the front of the vase.

7. Add the final palm frond on the left side, carefully angling it outward toward the front so that it sits up on the lip of the vase.

8. Add the willow branches so they shoot out between the palm fronds.

Peony and Rose Bouquet

What You'll Need

6 stems preserved pink rice flower

7 stems preserved dusty pink limonium

8 pink and red peonies (varying shades)

3 coral or salmon-pink roses

Frayed terra-cotta velvet ribbon

One of the most frequent questions I get is "What should I do with the special stems I've saved and dried from bouquets?" Instead of trying to re-create that keepsake arrangement, I think it's best to incorporate them into an entirely new bouquet that instantly turns into a conversation piece. You'll be able to point to individual ingredients and relay the story behind the stems.

I've used commonly saved flowers here (roses and peonies), but feel free to sub in your own keepsake materials.

1. Crisscross 3 stems of rice flower to form a tripod. These will act as the anchor stems.

2. Create depth by adding a few limonium just slightly above and next to the rice flower.

3. Add 5 peonies so that they pop out just slightly, evenly distributing them throughout the bouquet.

4. Layer in the remaining rice flower below the peonies to add both structure and depth. At this point, the bouquet should feel like it has a little bulk to it.

5. Add the remaining peonies, placing one low in front and one higher up in the back to create an overall sense of depth.

6. Add the roses throughout the bouquet, spacing them out so their colors are balanced across the arrangement.

7. Fill in around the roses with the remaining limonium, making sure there are a few taller pieces that stick out to add height and shape to the bouquet.

8. Trim all the stems to an even length. Tie off the bouquet with the ribbon.

NOTE: Refer to page 30 for a step-by-step look at creating a hand-tied bouquet.

All-Black Arrangement

What You'll Need

Widemouthed vase
Black floral spray paint
Chicken wire
10 to 12 stems preserved
    baby blue eucalyptus
9 stems purple dahlia
Black satin ribbon
    (optional)

If ever an arrangement conveyed a vibe, it's this one. Made specially for the goth girlies, this dark-hued arrangement is unapologetically moody.

Dahlias are notoriously difficult to work with, both fresh and dried, especially the larger ones, as their heads tend to fall off. (Insert Morticia Addams joke here.) For that reason, I use smaller varieties like *Dahlia pinnata* and dry them myself using the evaporation method (see page 33). If you're unable to source dahlias, substitute dark-colored roses or zinnias.

1. Use floral spray paint to slightly darken the eucalyptus. Let dry.

2. Insert your chicken wire into the vase, ensuring it doesn't peek over the edge.

3. Trim the tallest eucalyptus stem and place it in the center right, slightly toward the back. (This will act as the anchor stem.) Place shorter eucalyptus stems to the left and right.

4. Add 2 or 3 dahlia to the center so they pop out and over the eucalyptus. Place another dahlia low in the center front of the arrangement.

5. Continue adding shorter pieces of eucalyptus around the arrangement to fill in holes so you cannot see the chicken wire.

6. Add the remaining dahlia stems, varying their heights.

7. For a more feminine aesthetic, tie a long ribbon to each dahlia stem.

Cardoon, Statice, and Cecropia

What You'll Need

Large oblong pedestal vase
10 stems purple cardoon
Purple spray paint (optional)
Chicken wire
6 stems okra pods
10 to 15 stems light pink statice
6 stems dusty rose hanging amaranthus
1 cecropia leaf

Since flowers lose a lot of volume during the drying process, we are often left with skinny stems, and we overcompensate by stuffing our dried arrangements with too many flowers. This leads to bulky, overly vertical—and overly traditional—designs. Combining unusual ingredients like cardoon and okra in an asymmetrical arrangement immediately makes this lush design feel more contemporary, while tendrils of amaranthus add another layer of visual interest and sense of movement. Sourcing these harder-to-find ingredients may prove a bit difficult but will be well worth the effort. Check Etsy and flower farms that specialize in drying flowers. (See page 216 for a few sources I frequently purchase from.)

›› TURN THE PAGE TO
SEE HOW IT'S MADE

1. Lightly touch up the cardoon flower heads with spray paint if a stronger color is desired. (The ones shown here were spray-painted for a bolder look.) Let dry. Arrange the chicken wire in the vase so that it comes up just over the edge.

2. Trim 3 cardoon stems and place them on the right side of the vase at varying heights. Trim 2 okra pod stems and place one jutting out to the right of the cardoon and one at center left.

3. Trim 3 or 4 statice and add them around the cardoon to create a lush, full look. Place 2 additional okra pod stems on the left side of the arrangement, along with 2 cardoon in the low center left.

4. Trim 5 or 6 statice and add them along the front of the vase so they hang out. Add another cardoon on the right side of the arrangement.

5. Continue adding statice until all holes have been filled, except for a space for the cecropia leaf on the center left side. Layer amaranthus on the okra pods, draping the tendrils one by one so they loop and create a sense of overall movement.

6. Place the cecropia leaf at an angle in the remaining spot.

2

3

5

6

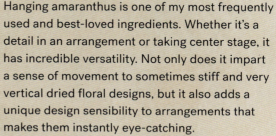

HANGING AMARANTHUS

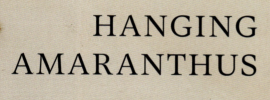

Hanging amaranthus is one of my most frequently used and best-loved ingredients. Whether it's a detail in an arrangement or taking center stage, it has incredible versatility. Not only does it impart a sense of movement to sometimes stiff and very vertical dried floral designs, but it also adds a unique design sensibility to arrangements that makes them instantly eye-catching.

You will frequently find amaranthus fresh at your local wholesaler or florist, and it can be easily air-dried (see page 32). If you're prioritizing sustainability, this will be the best route to go. However, it is important to note that the tendrils will shed any time they are touched, and the stem will become inflexible.

Hanging amaranthus is also available in preserved forms at specialty retailers such as Afloral and Etsy, in a range of bright and bold colors. I have used the preserved variety throughout this book; I find it really elevates and expands the design possibilities since the preserved plants retain their flexibility. But because the preserved type is a less sustainable option, I buy only what I am sure I need and reuse pieces from design to design when I am able.

Hanging Amaranthus Wreath

What You'll Need

12-inch (30 cm) premade
   grapevine wreath base
6 to 8 stems preserved
   green hanging
   amaranthus
Bind wire
3 stems preserved
   dark green upright
   amaranthus
Hot glue gun
3 dried oranges (whole,
   with leaves attached),
   or 3 dried orange slices

A few years ago I started adding hanging amaranthus to my custom wreaths for a dramatic effect, and I haven't looked back. You could say it's one of my signature designs.

When sourcing amaranthus, choose stems that have long, thick tendrils that can drape effectively and cover the wreath base. I recommend using a premade wreath base here because they tend to be sturdier overall and will hold and shape the tendrils of hanging amaranthus. (You can use one that you've constructed yourself, as explained on page 27; just be sure it is on the thicker, more supportive side.)

With a change of adornment (skip the oranges and add bells) this wreath also looks fantastic at the holidays.

1. Lay out the hanging amaranthus on top of the wreath base, planning which piece will go in which spot and making sure the tendrils drape along the curve of the wreath base. You may need more than one stem in each spot to cover the base and achieve the intended dramatic effect.

2. Remove the hanging amaranthus. Wrap the portion of the wreath base that will hold the hanging amaranthus with bind wire. Tightly tie it off on the back.

3. Slide the base of each hanging amaranthus stem under the bind wire. Drape the tendrils along the wreath base, making sure the smaller tendrils fall downward. Tuck the other end of each long hanging amaranthus stem underneath the bind wire to secure it in place.

4. Insert the upright amaranthus around the wreath base, equidistant from one another to add structure.

5. Hot-glue the oranges in the bottom right of the wreath base, nestling them into the amaranthus so they don't hang too far out.

NOTE: Refer to page 28 for more wreath-making guidance.

Painted Hydrangea and Curvy Sago Palm Fronds

What You'll Need

Medium jug
Hot pink, dark gold, and
    purple spray paints
3 sago palm fronds
9 stems hydrangea
    (rounded)
5 stems allium
Chicken wire
Thin-gauge wire (optional)

This entryway arrangement is based on a neutral one I designed for a client, turned up to 100. A wallflower it is not. Using an analogous color scheme (see page 24) imparts a harmonious feel, less Vegas showgirl and more design showstopper. The curvy sago palm fronds are key to the design but will probably be the hardest ingredient to source, as they are not usually dried in such a dramatic curved fashion. Check with your local specialty florist or source fresh sago palms and dry them yourself in any shape you wish by securing them with wire.

1. Paint the dried material: a medium coat of hot pink paint for the palm fronds, a light coat of dark gold paint for the hydrangea, and a medium coat of purple paint for the allium. Let dry.

2. Insert a small amount of chicken wire into the jug for stability.

3. Place the tallest, most striking palm frond in the center back, followed by the other two to the right of it. If need be, use wire to secure them to one another so they stand upright.

4. Trim the hydrangea and place seven of them to the left and center of the palm fronds. Place the remaining 2 hydrangea between the palm fronds on the right to create depth.

5. Trim the allium to varying heights and add them to the center.

← Saturating the allium flower heads with deep purple spray paint allows them to really pop against the hot pink sago palms.

↑ The dramatic snakelike shape of these sago palm fronds is achieved by tying the ends with a thin wire and letting the fronds air-dry.

Bold   57

Fuchsia Gomphrena and Pampas Grass Bouquet

What You'll Need

3 pampas grass plumes
3 stems strelitzia
15 to 20 stems fuchsia
   gomphrena
3 stems lotus seed pod
3 stems yellow strawflower
3 stems yellow craspedia
3 miscanthus plumes,
   leaves removed and
   reserved
Black satin ribbon

Since dried florals naturally lean boho, I wanted to give you a bolder, updated take on this style of bouquet. Here I use fluffy pampas grass plumes and sculptural strelitzia stems as the base of the bouquet, lending it structure as well as acting as a backdrop for the more colorful florals.

1. Hold the 3 plumes of pampas grass to form a tripod, with the tallest on the right and the shortest on the left. The tallest plume will sit in the center of the bouquet.

2. Add the strelitzia one at a time so that they crisscross with the pampas plumes, with the tallest strelitzia facing outward to the right. Place the remaining 2 strelitzia, one above and one below the initial strelitzia stem, also facing outward to balance the visual weight of the bouquet.

3. Add half of the gomphrena in the center of the bouquet.

4. Place a naturally forward-facing lotus seed pod low and centered in the bouquet. Add the tallest lotus seed pod in the center back, and nestle the remaining pod to the right between two strelitzia stems.

5. Add the rest of the gomphrena to the right side, below the strelitzia, taking care to place some under and around the lowest lotus seed pod so that there is a clear contrast between the two ingredients.

6. Add the miscanthus plumes so they fill out the space behind the strelitizia and craspedia. They will start to blend in with the pampas grass, creating a voluminous structure.

7. Put the strawflower on the left side to balance the weight of the bouquet. Some of the stems will move to the center as you adjust and add the others.

8. Add the craspedia at varying heights above the strawflower.

9. Add the miscanthus leaf with the most movement to the center front right so that it wraps around the strelitzia stems. Place 6 more miscanthus leaves throughout the bouquet to impart a sense of movement. (Your eye should move from leaf to leaf when looking at the bouquet.)

10. Trim the stems to an even length. Tie off the bouquet with the ribbon.

NOTE: Refer to page 30 for a step-by-step look at creating a hand-tied bouquet.

12-inch (30 cm) premade
straw wreath base
16 ounces (450 g) reindeer
moss
Floral pins
Bright blue spray paint
Frayed terra-cotta velvet
ribbon

Painted Reindeer Moss Wreath

A strategy I often employ is to use just one ingredient in an arrangement to defy any preconceived notions about dried florals. Instead of tired, lifeless flowers, a single material en masse creates a full, overflowing feel and dramatic effect. It's always striking and statement making.

This easy-to-replicate wreath is also an opportunity to play around with complementary color schemes (see page 24). Here I've chosen a bright sky blue for the base and paired it with a complementary dusty terra-cotta bow. If Smurf blue isn't your thing, though, I get it! Try this same technique using purple and yellow or red and green.

1. Place handfuls of reindeer moss on the wreath base, using floral pins to secure them, until the entire base is covered.

2. Paint the entire wreath until you achieve the desired color intensity. Let dry.

3. Tie a loopy ribbon bow and attach it to the top of the wreath with a floral pin.

Bold   61

Hanging Amaranthus Branch

What You'll Need

1 foraged branch
6 to 8 stems preserved
hanging amaranthus
(a mix of dark red and
dusty rose)
Hot glue gun
Fishing line or Command
medium wire toggle
hooks

This arrangement was originally conceived for a client with exquisite taste who was outfitting their modern country home with mostly vintage furniture. I needed a design that complemented the impeccable home décor. And so this dramatic branch installation was born.

Creating this piece changed how I thought and felt about my own floral designs. Of course they are considered a craft, but who's to say they aren't *art*? Although you can absolutely display this branch in a vase, hanging it from the ceiling or on the wall makes it feel more like an art installation.

Foraging for branches is a great way to find one that isn't stick-straight and has some movement, which will make the end result more interesting and eye-catching. Note that the length of the chosen branch will determine the number of hanging amaranthus stems you'll need.

1. Remove any small stems from the main branch with floral pruners.

2. Place the dark red amaranthus along the entire length of the branch, including any secondary offshoots.

3. Once you've determined the placement for all of the dark red amaranthus, secure it with hot glue. Hold the amaranthus down until the glue dries.

4. Repeat steps 2 and 3 with the dusty rose amaranthus, placing it directly next to the dark red amaranthus.

5. Brush out the amaranthus tendrils so that they drape downward.

6. Suspend from the ceiling with fishing line or hang on the wall using hooks.

Carlina Moon Flower and Tulip Cloche

What You'll Need

7-inch-tall (18 cm) glass
cloche
Pin frog
Floral putty
Spanish moss
Gloves
3 stems white carlina moon
flower
5 purple tulips with leaves
attached

Call it the grandmillennial home décor trend effect, but I've seen more and more cloches on display as of late. Not only do I find them to be a nostalgic inspiration, but they are a fantastic way to display more precious, finicky florals that need protection from touch. They can be obtained from many big-box retailers (the one used here is from IKEA).

Consider drying your own tulips using the air-drying method (see page 32), as they will be difficult to source. (I dried these myself and let them fall over the edge of the vase to achieve the curved stems.) Or substitute bendable, dyed dried grass.

1. Attach the pin frog to the base of the cloche with floral putty. Cover the frog with a few pieces of Spanish moss.

2. Carlina moon flowers are quite sharp, so be sure to wear gloves when working with them. Trim and insert the tallest moon flower toward the back of the frog, ensuring you've left enough space for the cloche to cover the arrangement.

3. Trim the second moon flower to approximately two-thirds the height of the tallest one and insert it in the center of the frog.

4. Trim the last moon flower to the base of the flower head and insert it at the front of the frog.

5. Place a curved tulip so it wraps around the top of the tallest moon flower and along the underside of the cloche's domed top.

6. Place a second tulip to sit low at the front of the cloche, and another toward the back left. Place the remaining tulips toward the back to fill in the space behind the moon flowers.

7. Tuck in any stems as needed to allow the cloche to comfortably cover the arrangement.

Painted Strelitzia and Bell Cups

What You'll Need

Square box planter
AgraWool block
Reindeer moss
Floral pins
Black floral spray paint
8 stems strelitzia
3 stems bell cups
Gold spray paint
5 stems lotus seed pod
11 to 13 dark red upright
    amaranthus
15 to 20 stems mini foxtail
    millet grass
15 to 20 stems lavender

Although flowers lose their heady aromas during the drying process, many retain a slight scent—including lavender. I included it in this design as an accent flower so its fragrance comes out without it taking over the aesthetic of the whole design. The gold-painted pieces and tall, dark stems of strelitzia add over-the-top depth, specially designed for those who follow the "more is more" motto. The black planter is also key to the drama here. If you can't find one that's dark enough, paint one with the same spray paint you use for the moss and strelitzia.

1. *If you're painting the planter*, place the AgraWool snugly inside. Attach the reindeer moss to the top of the AgraWool with floral pins. Use the floral spray paint to darken the moss and paint the outside of the planter. *If you don't want to paint the planter*, trim the AgraWool as necessary and attach the moss with pins away from the vessel. Paint the top of the moss-covered AgraWool and return it to the container once it has dried.

2. Paint the strelitzia black until you achieve an opaque coating; this will take two or three passes.

3. Paint the bell cups with a heavy coat of gold spray paint. Gently spray a light coat of gold across the tops of the lotus pods, focusing on the centers.

4. Turn the container so that a corner is facing you and place the 3 tallest, widest strelitzia in the center back. Trim the remaining strelitzia. Add 3 of the smaller stems on the right side and the other 2 stems on the left side, spacing them out.

5. Trim the bell cups quite short and add them at varying heights, stacking them up the center front of the arrangement.

6. Trim 3 lotus pods and add them around the bell cups. Place the rest of the lotus pods so they are gradually elevating toward the center of the arrangement.

7. Trim the amaranthus and add them along the back of the arrangement, just below the strelitzia.

8. To create additional color and depth, evenly distribute the mini foxtail at varying heights throughout the arrangement.

9. Add the lavender at varying heights throughout the arrangement, with a concentration at the center front.

↑ Choosing colorful stems in a range of hues adds to the dramatic feel of the arrangement, as do the different textures of each ingredient.

→ Concentrating the gold spray paint in the middle of the lotus seed pods gives the illusion of bright light dancing across the tops of the pods.

CALM

II.

If your interior design aesthetic can be described as clean and minimal, you love earth tones, and you consider your home your haven, this chapter is for you. The natural textures and colors of dried materials are on full display, imbuing each finished design with a sense of peacefulness. And because none of the materials in this chapter—with one exception—have been artificially treated, these projects are among the most sustainable in the book.

Many of the arrangements in this section, including sculptural branches and designs using dried grasses, are inspired by wabi-sabi and the art of ikebana. Finding the beauty in the imperfect and trying to facilitate a harmonious relationship between the design and the space it sits in were front of mind when I conceptualized these organic, free-flowing arrangements.

Large narrow-neck vase
5 stems kiwi vine
4 miscanthus plumes with
    leaves attached
¼ bunch light green soft
    wild grass

Sculptural Kiwi Vine and Grasses

Thoughtfully displayed branches have an inherent chicness, but the trick to making them look artful and intentional lies in your material selection. Any time you source branches, look for ones that have a bend or curve; stick-straight ingredients often make designs feel overly stiff.

For this project, look for kiwi vine stems with *lots* of variation in their shape and dried grasses that are soft and drape easily. Both elements will add visual interest and movement to the arrangement.

1. Choose the anchor stem of kiwi vine that you will design around. While this is often the tallest stem in an arrangement, here you'll want to choose a stem with lots of twirly and loopy details. Trim and place it in the center of the vase.

2. Add the remaining kiwi vines, trimming them as you go. Angle some to shoot outward, to capitalize on their curvy form.

3. Trim the miscanthus plumes and place them near the kiwi vines at varying heights.

4. Place a few stems of the soft wild grass in the center of the vase. Due to their soft, bendable nature, you will have to rest the grasses on the kiwi vines to achieve the organic look of blades of grass folding out and over the stems.

5. Add the remaining stems of the grass draping down the side of the vase.

Scabiosa Pods and Cress

12-inch-long (30 cm) piece
   chicken wire, at least
   6½ inches (17 cm) wide
12-by-4-inch (30 by
   10 cm) sheet cardboard
Floral tape
1 bunch light green soft
   wild grass
Zip ties
9 to 12 stems light green
   cress
7 stems poppy pods
10 to 15 stems natural or
   bleached bunny tails
5 stems preserved hanging
   amaranthus
5 stems scabiosa pods

Biophilic design is a concept used in architectural and building design that facilitates a connection with nature in the built environment. It is thought that this strategy has psychological benefits including reduced stress and improved cognitive function. On a smaller scale, plant-filled rooms bursting with greenery as an interior design aesthetic have undoubtedly had a resurgence in the past few years as many try to reap the benefits of this philosophy.

This design is my attempt to incorporate this concept into a dried floral arrangement. It's a tabletop installation that can be displayed on any flat surface and is light enough to easily move from place to place. Inspired by a windswept day at the beach, the piece has a gentle sense of movement that is calming and brings the outdoors in.

›› TURN THE PAGE TO
   SEE HOW IT'S MADE

1. Fashion the chicken wire into a 2-inch (5 cm) diameter tube and secure it to the cardboard with floral tape. (Placement of the tube does not need to be perfect; you just need to attach it to a flat surface.) Divide the soft wild grass into 4 smaller bunches and zip-tie each at its base to keep the stems together.

2. Place the first grass bunch in the center left of the chicken wire, inserting the stems so they are angled down and the top loops around the tube to cover the edge of the cardboard. Insert a second bunch of grass in the chicken wire on the left so it intersects with the top of the first bunch and the tail sweeps forward.

3. Repeat step 2 on the right side with the remaining grass bunches. You do not need to create an exact mirror image, but the placement should be similar, sitting slightly lower to cover the cardboard base.

4. Trim the cress stems and insert them at various angles throughout the base. The goal is to make it look a bit windswept. For additional texture, trim and add the poppy pods into the arrangement, three on one side and four on the other, sinking them low and close to the base.

5. Trim and place the bunny tails in the same manner as the cress.

6. Use the amaranthus to cover any holes or exposed chicken wire. Trim the scabiosa pods and insert them throughout the arrangement, angling them outward rather than straight up.

1
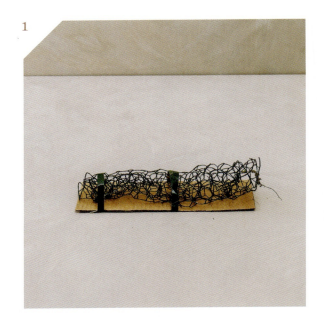

4

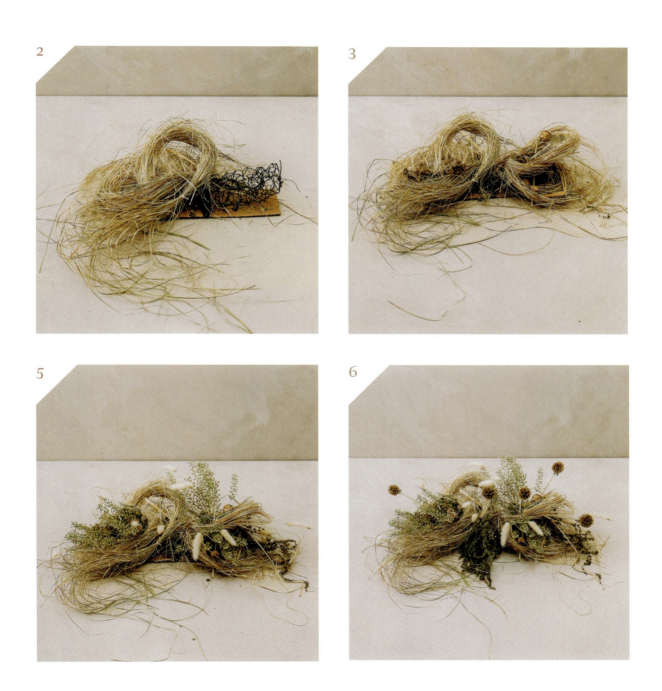

DRIED GRASSES

Grasses are one of my favorite materials, in part because there are so many different varieties, and also because their versatility allows me to create new shapes in arrangements and always sparks a creative idea, such as looping them in a wall hanging (see page 95). They imbue designs with a sense of movement, which can be challenging when working with dried material. And although they naturally dry in shades of green and brown, they manage to convey a sense of sophistication no matter where you use or display them. From my perspective, dried grasses instantly elevate my designs into the realm of art.

There are endless varieties to choose from, including bear grass, dune grass, wild grass, and ornamental meadow grass among many others, and of course pampas grass and miscanthus plumes. A quick online search is the best way I've found to source dried grasses aside from foraging for them, which I recommend doing in fall when they naturally start to dry out.

Sculptural Sarracenia

What You'll Need

Small pedestal vase
Pin frog
Floral putty
12 stems sarracenia
3 stems light green wild
    grass with long leaves
    and offshoots attached
3 stems clematis

Once I discovered that sarracenia (also called trumpet or pitcher plant) is easy to air-dry, I knew I had to create an arrangement that highlights its natural texture and color. You will likely have to dry these yourself (see page 32), as I have yet to find them available for purchase in a dried state. Although this process is fairly easy, they do become delicate and brittle, so be sure to prepare more than called for so that you have additional stems on hand if some break.

When sourcing wild grass, look for stems that have a few long leaves still attached. This is one of the few instances where I don't remove the dead leaves during processing but leave them on, as they add an extra artistic element to the overall design.

1. Adhere a pin frog to the inside of the vase with floral putty.

2. Place the tallest sarracenia in the back right of the pin frog. This will act as the anchor stem.

3. Trim the next tallest sarracenia and place it in the center of the pin frog. Continue trimming and adding stems around the center, using gradually shorter ones as you get farther from the center, to give the appearance they are growing up out of the vase.

4. Add the shortest piece of wild grass, with its leaves and offshoots attached, to the far left so it bends out of the vessel.

5. Trim the clematis to three different heights. Place the shortest one in the low front, the medium one in the center, and the tallest in back.

6. Place the next-tallest stem of wild grass, with its leaves and offshoots, just to the left of the tallest sarracenia.

7. Strip the leaves and offshoots from the longest and most dramatic bending stem of wild grass. Place it at the right side of the arrangement so it dramatically drapes out of the vessel.

← Display this arrangement in any room of the home, even (or especially) in the bathroom—it's picture-perfect resting here on a bathtub tray.

↓ The tips of the sarracenia get a little crispy and curl as they dry out, allowing their delicate, lacy veining to become all the more noticeable.

9 to 12 stems oleander
   seed pods
5 curly willow branches
5 stems inula
5 to 7 stems horsetail
   grass (stipa barba de
   bode)
Twine

Golden Curly Willow and Oleander Seed Pod Bouquet

Embracing the natural tones of dried materials that sometimes look withered is something I consider both a challenge and a benefit of working with these botanicals. I often think of one of the tenets of wabi-sabi—to embrace the beauty of things imperfect, impermanent, and incomplete—to help me wrap my head around how to create with dried flowers.

By leaning into a mahogany color palette for this bouquet, I can focus on the different natural textures and shapes: The curve of the oleander seed pod stems looks almost prehistoric, the horsetail grass reflects light brilliantly, and the inula heads look almost buttonlike.

1. Crisscross 3 oleander stems to form a tripod. These will act as the framework for the bouquet.

2. Add the longest curly willow branch directly in the center, shooting out of the bouquet.

3. Place 3 inula in the center of the bouquet, around the curly willow branch.

4. Add the rest of the oleander deep in front and on the right and left sides.

5. Place the remaining inula higher up in the bouquet, closest to the curly willow branch.

6. Add the shorter willow branches, focusing on the right side and arranging them so they jut out.

7. Place the horsetail grass in the center back so that it fills the space in the center of the bouquet.

8. Trim the stems to an even length. Tie off the bouquet with twine.

NOTE: Refer to page 30 for a step-by-step look at creating a hand-tied bouquet.

What You'll Need

Low bowl
Chicken wire
¼ bunch light green soft
    wild grass
Zip tie (optional)
½ bunch Indian ricegrass
10 to 15 stems mini foxtail
    millet grass

Loopy Dried Grasses

The first time I made an arrangement with a looped bunch of dried grass, it unlocked something in the artistic process for me. It felt inspiring to work with a material that can be manipulated into shapes and forms while still retaining its natural beauty.

Envisioned as a smaller tabletop arrangement for the bedroom or bathroom, this project easily adds visual interest to any room, bringing the outdoors in for a sense of calm. When sourcing your materials, test the grass for bendability, as it needs to be flexible.

›› TURN THE PAGE TO
SEE HOW IT'S MADE

1. Place chicken wire deep in the bowl.

2. Twist the soft wild grass so the ends are freely hanging out and you've created a vertical loop. Stuff the gathered ends into the chicken wire so the loop drapes over the side of the vase. (For a tighter loop, secure with a zip tie so that it will not move once placed in the bowl.)

3. Insert a few of the tallest pieces of ricegrass on a diagonal from the top center right down to the center of the bowl. Add a few shorter pieces on the left side to balance the visual weight of the arrangement.

4. Trim the remaining ricegrass and place it at lower heights, splaying outward.

5. Place the tallest stem of mini foxtail alongside the tallest piece of ricegrass. Trim the remaining mini foxtail stems and evenly distribute them among the ricegrass.

6. Trim any errant grass pieces from the arrangement once the design is completed.

1

4

Cress and Poppy Pod Bouquet

What You'll Need

¼ bunch light green soft
   wild grass
Zip tie
9 stems light green cress
5 stems poppy pods
5 stems Indian ricegrass
Twine

In exploring the versatility and flexibility of dried grasses, I landed on creating a nontraditional petite posy featuring looped grass and poppy pods that would make an excellent bridesmaid bouquet for a beach destination wedding or summer holiday hostess gift. The subdued, monochromatic color palette (see page 24) puts the focus on the texture and movement of each material in this small but statement-making bouquet. You could also experiment with adding another dried grass loop or even a braid of grass to take it to a higher level of visual interest.

1. Create a small loop with the soft wild grass, connecting it back to where you are holding it. Use a zip tie to secure the loop. Think of it as the framework for the bouquet, to which you will secure other stems.

2. Add the cress into and around the loop by sticking them through different sections, four on one side and five on the other.

3. Add the poppy pods, keeping three farther out above the cress and pushing two deeper into the bouquet.

4. Position the ricegrass around the perimeter to add a sense of movement.

5. Trim the stems to an even length. Secure the bouquet and tie a bow with twine.

NOTE: Refer to page 30 for a step-by-step look at creating a hand-tied bouquet.

1 bunch light green soft
  wild grass
1 large foraged branch
Zip ties
2 milkweed pod branches
Small Command wire
  toggle hook or nail

Branch and Grass Wall Hanging

I often collect sticks and branches that I think have potential for future design projects. The requirements for these branches aren't strict—they just need to look interesting, and bonus points if they have a curve or bend. Selecting the perfect branch will be vital to the success of this wall hanging. I recommend using one that is about 1 inch (2.5 cm) in diameter and has a slight bend.

1. Loosely loop the soft wild grass around the center of the branch, ideally at a point where the branch bends. The base of the grass should lie against the underside of the branch, and the tail of the grass should drape down alongside the branch. Hold the base in place against the branch while you adjust the loop in front to your liking. Secure the base of the grass to the branch with a zip tie so that the tie is hidden by the loop on the front (see left).

2. Place the milkweed branches alongside the top of the branch so they appear to be coming out of the looped grass. Secure both in place with a single zip tie.

3. Angle a bit of the grass tail upward so that it drapes over the branch. Secure it with a zip tie behind the loop. Cut off the excess ends of all the zip ties.

4. To hang, attach the Command hook or nail to the wall. (I recommend using a Command hook because it will more easily and securely hold a zip tie.) Hang the arrangement on the zip tie attached to the base of the grass on the branch.

2 small shallow bowls
2 small pin frogs
Floral putty
6 stems scabiosa pods

Complementary Scabiosa Pod Stems

The art of ikebana takes decades to master. It emphasizes simplicity and understated elegance, playing with asymmetry and negative space to highlight the natural beauty of flowers. Like many floral designers, I am continually inspired by this art form and try to incorporate its characteristics in my own work, including this very simple but statement-making arrangement.

Sourcing stems that have a slight bend or curve will be crucial to achieving the eye-catching look of this project. I've found it difficult to find pre-dried scabiosa pod stems that are not super straight, so I recommend buying fresh scabiosa and drying them yourself. Use the evaporation technique (see page 33) and leave them in a vase with a wide mouth so they naturally drape over the side and dry with a bend in the stem.

1. Adhere a pin frog inside each bowl with floral putty.

2. Lay out the scabiosa pods so that you can identify those with the most bend or movement to their stems.

3. For the first bowl: Place the scabiosa with the most dramatic curve in the pin frog, angling it outward to the right. Trim a second stem to approximately two-thirds the height of the first and place it to the left of the first, angling it out to the left. Trim a third stem to approximately one-third the height of the tallest stem and place it low in the center right of the pin frog.

4. As you begin filling the second bowl, keep in mind that you want the two arrangements to complement each other when sitting side by side. Place a scabiosa with an interesting bend on the left side of the pin frog, arranged so that it will cozily fit into the nook of the stems in the first bowl. Trim a second stem slightly shorter than the first and place it on the right side. Trim the remaining stem to approximately two-thirds the height of the tallest stem and place it in the center front.

Foraged Leaves and Miscanthus Meadow

What You'll Need

2 AgraWool blocks
12-by-12-inch
  (30-by-30 cm) plate
  galvanized steel
  (28 gauge)
Floral tape
1 bunch bear grass
8 tall miscanthus plumes
  with leaves attached
½ bunch golden dune
  grass
6 stems ammi
10 to 15 stems bracken
  fern, plus more for
  covering base (optional)
Foraged leaves

Designed to bring the outdoors inside, this peaceful meadow installation is easier to create than you might think at first glance. It will require a trip to the hardware store, but nothing makes you feel more legit as a designer than using building materials for your creations. The galvanized steel plate primarily serves to weight down the arrangement, which is necessary since you are using taller-than-average plants that tend to topple over. If you do not have AgraWool blocks on hand, you can use any number of materials you may have, including hay bricks, a block of leftover packing foam, or floral foam. (For sustainability reasons I don't recommend buying new floral foam, but if you happen to have some left over from another project, you can use it here.)

1. Place the AgraWool blocks next to each other in the center of the steel plate. Wrap floral tape around the blocks and steel plate multiple times to ensure that they will not move.

2. Place the bear grass evenly throughout the blocks, pressing the bases of the stems in deeply.

3. Insert the tallest miscanthus in the center left. Trim the rest of the miscanthus and evenly distribute them throughout the arrangement. Add shorter pieces in the center front.

4. Trim the dune grass and insert it, evenly distributing shorter and taller pieces throughout.

5. Trim 3 ammi and place them in the front, one down low and the other two so they appear to be growing out of the base.

6. Place the bracken fern in the low front and around the low back to ensure that the base is covered.

7. Place the remaining ammi in the center back.

8. Once the arrangement is installed where you want it, cover the base with foraged leaves, taking care to make the leaves appear as though they're organically nestled around it. You can also use more bracken fern if you're not able to source crisp fallen leaves.

← Forage the biggest golden leaves you can find during the peak autumn season so that they will easily cover the structural base.

↑ Delicate miscanthus plumes add airiness to the installation and will gently sway every time someone walks by.

Medium narrow-neck vase
7 to 9 stems oleander seed
   pods
5 to 7 stems natural
   horsetail grass (stipa
   barba de bode)
7 stems clematis
2 curly willow branches

Golden Oleander Seed Pods and Clematis

Calming sepia tones are on display in this tabletop arrangement designed to add a golden glow to any room. It would be equally at home in cottagecore décor or a modern, minimalist setting, depending on the style of vessel you choose. The most important thing is that it have a narrow neck since there are no additional support mechanisms.

Oleander seed pods grow in different directions and are twisty by nature, so when you process these stems, leave only the top seed heads in place and remove the rest from the stem. And a few pieces of horsetail grass go a long way, so you don't need to add many to make an impact.

1. Place the tallest oleander stem on the right side of the vase (trim it if necessary for it to stay upright). Trim and place a second stem to the left of center.

2. Trim 2 or 3 shorter oleander stems and place them down low in front. Continue placing the rest of these stems on both sides of the vase, angling out where possible.

3. Add a few stems of horsetail grass in and around the oleander, concentrating on the left side.

4. Trim the clematis and add them to the center of the vase, placing the tallest in the center and the shorter ones closer to the rim of the vessel.

5. Place the curly willow branches just behind the tallest oleander, to add height to the arrangement.

6. Add the remaining horsetail grass, filling in toward the center.

JOYFUL

III.

Dried—nay, *dead*—flowers for a celebration?! Yes, it can be done, and with stunning results. With a little paint and thoughtful execution, you can upend expectations of what dried florals can be. This chapter is filled with bright blooms meant to lift your spirits and serve as the perfect focal point for your next celebratory event. From a playful bouquet that will brighten your day to a Barbie-inspired tabletop arrangement, the projects that follow are designed for happiness and joy.

What You'll Need

10 to 15 stems fresh
  baby's breath per cloud
Bright yellow, pink, and/or
  bright blue spray paint
Chicken wire
Fishing line (optional)

Baby's Breath Mini Clouds

A fun design to incorporate into your next event or install above a crib as a mobile. Baby's breath is one of the few materials I've found that you can work with before it's fully dried—in fact, it's easier to paint and manipulate when it's fresh. It will naturally dry on its own in the form you've installed it in. The only thing to consider when going this route is that you will need to slightly overstuff the clouds, as the stems will naturally lose volume as they dry out.

1. Paint the baby's breath flower heads in your choice of color(s). These will absorb a lot of paint, so be prepared to do multiple coats to achieve a bright color intensity. Let dry.

2. Roll a tight 2- to 3-inch (5 to 7.5 cm) diameter ball of chicken wire for each cloud. Remember: The larger the ball, the larger the cloud will be.

3. Begin stuffing a few stems of baby's breath into the chicken wire at a time, trimming them short as you go.

4. Continue covering the chicken wire ball all the way around. The trickiest part of this arrangement is evenly distributing the flowers, taking care not to have any stems poking out.

5. Repeat steps 2 through 4 for any additional clouds.

6. Once the clouds are complete, spray a final coat of paint on each to ensure a bright overall color.

7. If hanging, attach fishing line to the center of the cloud by stringing it through an opening in the chicken wire and tying it off with multiple knots. (I recommend testing the exact spot where it will hang beforehand, as the cloud will move and sway if hung in a drafty location.)

NOTE: This same process can be used to create any type of cloud installation—just increase the size of the chicken wire ball for larger clouds and/or if you're incorporating heavier materials.

Banksia and Palms

What You'll Need

Large round narrow-neck
   vase
Rust, bright yellow, and
   medium green spray
   paint
3 stems banksia
2 sago palm fronds
1 areca palm frond
5 stems strelitzia
5 stems leucadendron

I often like to play with scale when I want to make a dramatic statement. The trick to making this work in an overall design is to ensure it feels balanced. In this arrangement, I'm using extra-tall sago palms that jut out of the top of the vessel. To balance this verticality, I've placed banksia stems low so they spill out of and down the front of the vase to visually anchor the arrangement. I've also chosen a wide round vessel with a narrow neck, which supports the tall stems and helps balance the overall look of the arrangement by adding bulk at the bottom. Carefully choosing a vessel with your specific design in mind, instead of trying to make any flowers work in any vase, will elevate the look of all of your arrangements.

1. Paint the banksia heads rust and their tendrils green, the sago palm fronds bright yellow, and the areca palm frond green. The paint is meant to simply amp up the existing colors, so a light coat will suffice.

2. Paint the strelitzia bright yellow. After they have dried, go back over them with a light mist of rust to impart a bit of depth on each stem.

3. After all of the material has dried, layer the banksia on top of one another toward the left of the vessel opening. You will likely not need to trim these stems if using a large vessel, as these are typically short. You may need to trim some of the green tendrils off the stems, though.

4. Add the sago palm fronds in the center back, angling them off to the side, with the tallest toward the center of the arrangement. At this point the stems may feel a little loose in the vessel; you'll likely need to shift them back into place as you add the rest of the materials.

5. Trim the strelitzia and add two of the most striking stems to the left of the taller sago palm frond. Place the remaining strelitzia to the right, angling them out to convey a sense of movement.

6. Add the leucadendron in the center, angling them out toward the right. Again, you will likely not need to trim these stems, as they tend to be short.

7. Add the areca palm frond to the back left, behind the banksia, to fill in that side of the arrangement.

↑ Applying a light coat of spray paint to the banksia and strelitzia stems restores them to their peak color, which often fades during the drying process.

→ Leucadendron are nestled into the arrangement to balance its visual weight and add a moment of playfulness. Gently push the leaves back on the flower heads to help open them up.

Medium pitcher
40 to 50 stems purple
  statice
Floral tape or rubber bands

Purple Statice

This project is designed to look as though you effortlessly brought in colorful stems from the garden, put them in a pitcher, and let them dry naturally. The most critical part of this arrangement will be the prep work for the stems, which, while time-consuming, will produce colorful results. Since statice have multiple flower heads on each stem that tend to face in different directions, you'll trim the smaller pieces off the main stem and then group them together, facing the same direction, to achieve the maximum color impact in the arrangement.

1. For each statice, trim the offshoots from the main stem. Bundle the smaller pieces alongside the longer ones so the heads all face the same direction (for more on bundling, see page 19). Tape the pieces together using floral tape. (You can use rubber bands instead, but they will add bulk to each bundle, which can make it difficult to put them in the pitcher together.) Vary the placement of the smaller stems around each main one, and create bundles of different heights and widths to give them an organic feel.

2. Once you're finished prepping all the statice, plan the shape you want to achieve. (I've chosen an asymmetrical triangular shape here, as it mirrors the shape of my pitcher, but you can design to another shape.) Place one of the tallest bundles in the pitcher to serve as the anchor stem.

3. One by one, place the bundles in the pitcher, slowly building out the shape you want to achieve. Depending on the size of the pitcher, the bundles may shift around, but as you continue to add more, they will hold one another up.

4. Fill in any holes to achieve a uniform appearance.

STATICE

Often overlooked as just a filler flower, statice is sturdy and easy to source, and retains its bright, joyous color even after drying. It never ceases to amaze me just how vibrant dried statice are when I go to arrange with them. I like to think that I am helping give this underappreciated flower its due by featuring it frequently in my designs. (See pages 46, 115, 121, and 124 for projects featuring statice.)

Statice is also shockingly easy to dry on your own: Just leave it in a vase or bucket to air-dry over a few weeks (see page 32 for more on this method). I find that thoroughly processing it after it has dried, by removing all leaves and extraneous secondary stems and leaving only the top flower head, allows this material to really come to life. I recommend that you wait to process these stems until after they dry because you will likely want to keep the small offshoot stems for detail work in wreaths, bouquets, tabletop arrangements— anywhere that needs a bright pop of color.

Painted Hydrangea and Magnolia Nutshell

What You'll Need

Medium pedestal vase
Light pink and fuchsia
    spray paints
Pin frog
Floral putty
Chicken wire
10 to 15 stems hydrangea
    (a mix of round and
    vertical)
5 stems magnolia nutshell
    flower (see Note,
    page 130)
6 to 8 stems Indian
    ricegrass

I believe there are two kinds of people in this world: people who absolutely love pink and those who don't. I fall into the latter camp, but I would be remiss if I didn't include this bright pink Barbie-inspired arrangement for lovers of the feminine hue. And a note for my fellow pink-averse out there: This design can be completed in shades of any color and will achieve a similar striking result.

1. Paint all the materials: light pink for the magnolia nutshells and ricegrass, and fuchsia for the hydrangea. (The hydrangea will likely absorb a lot of the paint and need a few coats.) Let dry.

2. Adhere a pin frog to the inside of the vase with floral putty. Add chicken wire on top for additional support. Squish the chicken wire down below the lip of the vase so it's not visible.

3. Trim 2 vertical hydrangea and place them in the center back, orienting them toward either side.

4. Trim 2 round hydrangea and add them to the front, angling them out and down.

5. To help you orient the placement of all the magnolia nutshells, trim the first one and place it in the low front center, adjusting it so sits upward. Trim the remaining magnolia nutshells and add them to the left and right of center, nestling them in between the hydrangea. These are the focal points of the arrangement, so take some time to adjust them until they form a triangular shape within the arrangement.

6. Place the remaining hydrangea around the arrangement, trimming each stem as you go and evenly distributing the weight within it.

7. Use the ricegrass to fill in any holes and add visual interest. (I find that a little goes a long way.)

NOTE: Take care when placing the hydrangea. They are top-heavy, and the flower heads balancing on skinny, brittle stems are prone to snapping.

Purple Limonium and Blue Thistle

What You'll Need

Small widemouthed vase
Chicken wire
10 to 15 stems blue statice
20 to 25 stems light purple limonium
12 to 15 stems medium blue thistle
10 to 12 stems light blue globe thistle
11 stems dahlia (in various analogous shades; see page 24)
1 stem light pink strawflower
5 to 8 curly willow branches

This design started as a fun challenge for myself, to give new life to the dense, traditional dried floral arrangements of decades past. To do so, I started with classic flower choices but arranged them in a new way, incorporating dahlias into an asymmetrical, ombré design. It's still a lush, full arrangement but aligns a bit better with contemporary tastes.

With the exception of the dahlias, you can probably find these materials at your local grocery store. I recommend using a smaller dahlia variety like *Dahlia pinnata*; you can also use roses if you can't source dahlias. Additionally, if you're not able to find the variety of colors needed to achieve the ombré effect, complete the design with dahlias in complementary shades of orange and pink.

›› TURN THE PAGE TO
SEE HOW IT'S MADE

1. Insert a ball of chicken wire into the vase. Wrap it a few times, as the denser the ball of chicken wire, the denser the design will be. Choose 1 statice to act as the anchor stem, around which you will build out the rest of the arrangement.

2. Trim the limionium and begin adding them around the anchor stem so that they gradually splay out around it. Since limonium is fluffy, I recommend adding one at a time to avoid overstuffing.

3. Trimming each stem as you go, add more statice in the same areas as the limonium, with a concentration near the center to create a lusher, more colorful arrangement.

4. Place both varieties of thistle along the edges of the arrangement to add more texture.

5. If you have a variety of shades of dahlia, add them from right to left, going from lightest to darkest and distributing them throughout. Concentrate the majority of the blooms in the center.

6. Add the lightest-colored flower you have (in this case, the strawflower) to the outermost edge on the right side. To create a sense of movement within the arrangement, concentrate the squiggliest willow branches on the right side.

2

3

5

6

What You'll Need

12 to 15 stems white
statice
5 stems golden yarrow
12 dark purple spray roses
10 to 12 stems purple
nigella
Twine or ribbon

Purple Nigella and Golden Yarrow Bouquet

This updated take on the sweet, sentimental everlasting garden bouquet features commonly grown farm flowers, making it a good option if you want to prioritize sustainability and minimize environmental impact. Look for yarrow, nigella, and statice at your local farmers' market (see page 32 for tips on how to dry them yourself). Tying off the bouquet with twine is a great sustainable choice, but a satin or silk ribbon will make it feel fancier.

1. Statice has smaller offshoots with flower heads that grow below the "main" flower head. Remove these offshoots so that you have a single flower left on each stem.

2. Crisscross the stems of 3 yarrow to form a tripod. These will act as the anchor.

3. To create depth, add 3 statice so they are just slightly above and next to the yarrow.

4. Evenly distribute 4 to 6 roses throughout the bouquet, arranging them so they pop out just slightly.

5. Layer in 4 to 6 statice below the roses to add both structure and depth.

6. At this point, the bouquet should feel like it has a little bulk to it. Add the remaining 2 yarrow, placing one low in front and one higher up in the back of the bouquet.

7. Add a few nigella next to the roses so they pop out.

8. Add the remaining roses, spreading them throughout the bouquet to keep the eye moving and add visual interest.

9. Fill in around the roses with the remaining statice.

10. Carefully add the remaining nigella stems. Note that at this point the bouquet will be tightly packed together and it will become harder to insert the remaining stems without breaking them, so proceed carefully.

11. Trim all of the stems to an even length. Tie off the bouquet.

NOTE: Refer to page 30 for a step-by-step look at creating a hand-tied bouquet.

Strawberry and Saffron Wreath

What You'll Need

10-inch (25 cm) premade
grapevine base (or
create your own; see
page 27)
35 to 45 stems golden
solidago
25 to 35 stems red-orange
gomphrena
16 stems white winged
everlasting
Paddle wire or bind wire

How to create a traditional, lush wreath is one of the first things I learned when I started in floral design. Wreaths make excellent gifts—the perfect balance of thoughtful and ready to use. And I find that I can put my own design spin on them simply by using an unexpected color palette. Here I've essentially chosen the infamous ketchup-and-mustard combo that really took hold of millennials in the late aughts—but done with dried flowers, the pairing feels sweet and unexpected.

1. Create 16 small bundles, each containing a mix of all the materials: Take a few solidago and layer a few gomphrena on top, followed by one small stem of the winged everlasting. Secure the bundle with a twist of wire and trim the stems short.

2. Lay the bundles on top of the wreath base to see how they will look together. Make adjustments or change the order if necessary.

3. Once you've made any desired tweaks, place the first bundle on the wreath base and wrap the stems with paddle wire to secure it. I like to wrap the initial bundle a few times to ensure it will not move.

4. Continue layering the bundles on top of one another, working your way around the base and securing each with wire, taking care to wrap only the stem portion of each bundle.

5. Insert the stems of the last bundle under the very first bundle you attached, gently nestling it in place so that it completes the circle. This last bundle will likely need some zhuzhing to make it fit seamlessly.

6. Tie off and cut the wire on the back of the wreath.

7. Fill in any gaps or holes in the wreath by tucking leftover stems into the base. Pay attention to the overall placement of the ingredients to ensure the design feels balanced, with each variety evenly distributed throughout the wreath.

NOTES: If you're making your own wreath base, you may need slightly more or less of each ingredient. Refer to page 28 for more wreath-making guidance.

Each winged everlasting stem contains multiple offshoots, so be sure to snip these off so that they are evenly dispersed throughout the design.

Rudbeckia and Palm Frond Bouquet

What You'll Need

1 palm frond
Light green spray paint
10 to15 stems mini foxtail
    millet grass
3 stems silver brunia
5 stems globe thistle
5 miscanthus plumes,
    leaves removed and
    reserved
8 stems rudbeckia
Gold wired ribbon

What would I bring to a Barefoot Contessa–inspired seaside luncheon? This easy, breezy bouquet, which manages to feel both effortless with wild miscanthus plumes and a little fancy thanks to the gold ribbon. Reminiscent of a black-eyed Susan, rudbeckia is a fragile stem, easy to accidentally decapitate, so handle it with care. For a heartier and easier-to-find swap, sunflowers also work perfectly in this bouquet.

1. Give the palm frond a light coating of paint. Let dry.

2. Holding the palm frond, which will act as the anchor stem, add 3 or 4 mini foxtails, loosely placing them in front of the palm frond.

3. Place 1 silver brunia toward the center front of the bundle. Add the remaining silver brunia behind the first; this will create a support system for the rest of the stems.

4. Continue adding mini foxtail in a crisscross fashion to create density and texture in the bouquet.

5. Place the globe thistle in the bouquet, concentrated near the front.

6. Fill in any holes with miscanthus plumes.

7. Carefully place the rudbeckia at varying heights throughout the bouquet to add a pop of bright color.

8. Add 4 miscanthus leaves to the sides of the bouquet to impart a sense of movement.

9. Trim all of the stems to an even length. Tie off the bouquet with the ribbon.

NOTE: Refer to page 30 for a step-by-step look at creating a hand-tied bouquet.

Golden Yarrow and Ferns

What You'll Need

Medium pedestal vase
Hairpin frog
Floral putty
Light rust and golden
    yellow spray paints
5 stems bracken fern
5 stems magnolia nutshell
    flowers (see Note)
3 tall stems yellow
    eremurus
12 to 15 stems golden
    yarrow (varying sizes of
    flower heads and stems)

Yellow is often thought to be the most joyous color (just think of the iconic smiley face), so when I designed this arrangement I figured utilizing this happy hue in an analogous color scheme (see page 24) would produce equally happy results. Envisioned as the perfect gift for a fashionable friend who has an eye for interior design, this arrangement is best suited for a location where it will have maximum visibility, like an entryway or dining table.

Note: This project calls for magnolia nutshell flowers, which are neither flowers nor nutshells—they're the pods of magnolia flower heads that have been glued together. You can find both natural and painted versions on Etsy.

›› TURN THE PAGE TO
   SEE HOW IT'S MADE

1. Paint the bracken ferns light rust and the magnolia nutshell flower heads golden yellow. I recommend doing a light spray on the ferns so that they have a bright wash of color across the surface. For the magnolia nutshell, continue painting until you achieve a uniform bright yellow. Place a hairpin frog in the vase and adhere it with floral putty.

2. Trim the eremurus and place the tallest stem in the center of the frog to act as an anchor point for the arrangement. Add 2 shorter eremurus to the left and right of the anchor stem, angling the tips outward.

3. Select 3 or 4 of the bigger-headed yarrow and trim them so they will sit just above the lip of the vase. Place them to the left of the anchor stem.

4. Trim 3 or 4 more yarrow and add them near the center of the arrangement, angling them to cover the frog. Cut 1 magnolia nutshell to a similar length as the yarrow and place it to the right of the yarrow. Trim another magnolia nutshell and set it to the left. Adjust and separate the eremurus so that the stems on the right and left gently lean to their respective sides.

5. Trim the remaining 2 magnolia nutshells and place them at varying heights around the arrangement. Angle them in the frog so they appear to pop out.

6. Place the ferns in the holes of the arrangement, angling one down and out of the vessel in front, one on each side, and the remaining two on either side of the anchor stem. Keep the remaining yarrow stems long and place them so they shoot out of the sides of the arrangement, facing outward.

1

4

2

3

5

6

Pink Delphinium Wreath

What You'll Need

Handmade asymmetrical
 grapevine wreath base
 (see page 27)
Bind wire
30 to 35 stems pink
 delphinium
6 stems preserved light
 pink tiki fern
1 stem pincushion protea
Dusty rose silk ribbon

An easy way to make a wreath design really stand out is to make it asymmetrical. A full circle wreath feels traditional, sophisticated, adult. But an asymmetrical pink wreath? Instantly youthful, fun, and energetic. (It also makes a great baby shower decoration, by the way.)

Look to Etsy to source preserved tiki fern, or substitute dried needle grass for a similar effect. Additionally, if you're opting for a premade wreath base, be sure that one side is wider than the other, as it will help balance the overall look and feel of the final design.

1. Wrap the portion of the wreath base that will be covered by florals with bind wire. Tightly tie it off on the back.

2. Create the first few bundles by layering 4 or 5 delphinium on top of a few wisps of the tiki fern. Note that I skip the step of tying off each bundle here because they will be securely held by the wire wrapping on the base.

3. Mock up the wreath by laying the bundles on the base, taking care to leave the widest part free of any materials. This will help achieve a more evenly weighted final design.

4. Choose the point where the pincushion protea and ribbon will go. Placing the pincushion protea to the left instead of dead center will help to make the asymmetry pleasing to the eye. Once you've determined the spot, trim the stem and place it in the base under the wire wrapping. (I like to add the ribbon at the end so it doesn't tangle with any other materials while working with them.)

5. Create 2 more bundles that will splay outward from the protea in opposite directions. Slide them into place on the base.

6. To help ensure a perfectly offset final look for this asymmetric design, continue to create a few bundles at a time and check their placement as you go.

7. Once you've made all the bundles, slide them into place underneath the wire wrapping on the base.

8. Tie the ribbon in a very loopy bow and attach the knot underneath the edge of the base with bind wire so that the ends flow down.

NOTE: Due to the handmade nature of the wreath base, you may need slightly more or less of each ingredient. Refer to page 28 for more wreath-making guidance.

WISTFUL

IV.

If you're anything like me, nostalgia tugs at your heartstrings any time you see something that reminds you of your childhood. Dried flowers remind me of my grandmother's home, where, faded from the sun, they were tucked into small vases and never ceased to capture my attention. Every dried flower comes with a story, a history, and this inherent nostalgia is what I believe draws the hopeless romantic, the coquette, and the cottagecore-obsessed to dried floral design.

I'm leaning into that wistful romance here, with projects that highlight the feminine, ethereal quality of dried flowers, including a bridal-inspired bouquet; a wispy, free-flowing tabletop design; everlasting flowering branches; and a wreath featuring delicate ingredients that seem to float on air.

Lunaria and Ranunculus Bouquet

What You'll Need

7 to 9 stems lunaria seed
    pods, seeds and husks
    removed
5 stems bleached
    helichrysum
    (immortelle)
7 stems yellow ranunculus
12 to 15 stems white
    xeranthemum
Long tan silk gossamer
    ribbon

I often get requests for bridal bouquets for destination weddings and elopements, arrangements built to withstand shipping but elegant enough to complement a bridal look. This is the style of bouquet I turn to time and time again to get the job done. Sweet, delicate ranunculus blooms provide a nice pop of color but can easily be omitted for an all-white look.

White xeranthemum are a critical component of this bouquet, as they add an ethereal quality with a sense of movement. These stems can be a challenge to source, but I've always had luck finding them online at Charles Little and Co., so I recommend you start your search there.

1. Hold 3 lunaria, including the tallest stem, in one hand in a crisscross fashion to form a tripod.

2. Place 3 helichrysum low down between the lunaria. These will help create the structure to hold the more delicate blooms.

3. Add 3 more lunaria, evenly distributing them throughout the bouquet.

4. Place the remaining 2 helichrysum so they sit just above the initial helichrysum, creating a sense of depth when you look at the bouquet from above.

5. Add the first few ranunculus above the helichrysum so their color pops against the white backdrop.

6. Insert the remaining lunaria so their overall visual weight is balanced throughout.

7. Add 5 xeranthemum so they shoot out of the bouquet, adding a sense of movement.

8. Place the remaining ranunculus at various heights throughout the bouquet, keeping their heads above the helichrysum.

9. Add the remaining xeranthemum above and around the ranunculus.

10. Trim the stems to an even length. Tie off the bouquet with the ribbon for a romantic effect.

NOTE: Refer to page 30 for a step-by-step look at creating a hand-tied bouquet.

Everlasting Flowering Branches

What You'll Need

Tall narrow-neck jug or
    vase
3 thin branches of differing
    lengths
Hot glue gun (see Note)
20 to 30 strawflower
    heads

The epitome of spring, flowering branches can last all year long in this easy yet impactful arrangement. Material selection is key here: Be sure to choose relatively slim, delicate branches when foraging and/or sourcing. The ones I used here were collected in early spring and have tiny leaves on them, giving them the natural look and growth of a flowering branch.

1. Play with the placement of the branches by setting them in the jug and seeing how they naturally rest before deciding on the final height of each; you'll ultimately want one to be very tall, one medium, and one short. Trim each branch and return them to the jug.

2. One by one, place a dot of hot glue on the branches where you want to attach a strawflower head and immediately press the underside of a flower into the glue. Hold it there until the glue dries. Leave the smallest flower heads for the tops of the branches. The overall look should be organic, as though the branch has just started to flower, so you'll want to place the strawflower in different areas of the branches. Don't get too hung up on placement, as you can always pop a flower head off once the glue is dry and reglue it in a new spot.

3. Once all the strawflower heads are attached and you have transferred the arrangement to its final location, adjust the branches so they are evenly spaced, imparting a sense of airiness between them.

NOTE: You can use fine metal wire to wrap the flower heads if you're not inclined to use hot glue.

↑ Look for thin, flexible branches with tiny leaves to help create the impression that they were foraged in early spring.

→ Choosing strawflower heads of different sizes and varying their placement from branch to branch will lend an organic feel to the arrangement.

STRAWFLOWER

This widely available flower is one of the most popular in dried floral design, for good reason: It's sturdy, it's easy to dry, and it retains its color beautifully. The rainbow of natural color options to choose from is far more extensive than most other dried flower varieties. Also, it is often available at local flower farms and growers, making it a sustainable choice. Look for it at farmers' markets as well.

As you search for strawflowers, you'll discover that this name is applied to a few different varieties of similar-looking flowers in the Asteraceae family, such as *Helichrysum vestitum* and *Xerochrysum bracteatum*, all of which have fluffy, often colorful heads with sturdy stems.

Although they tend to have shorter stems, these flowers work well in almost all dried floral projects, from bouquets and wreaths to tabletop designs. They can do it all, and I have featured them in nearly every type of arrangement in this book!

If you're just starting to work with dried flowers, this will be a versatile ingredient to have on hand. And if you want to try your hand at drying them at home, you'll be pleased with how easily you can do this. I recommend processing each bunch and leaving it to hang-dry (see page 33) for a few weeks. You'll come back to fully dried flowers ready for design work.

Blush Leather Fern and Winged Everlasting Bouquet

What You'll Need

3 stems preserved blush
    leather fern
5 stems bleached,
    preserved rice flower
5 to 7 stems bleached,
    preserved limonium
7 stems bleached,
    preserved craspedia
5 to 7 stems white winged
    everlasting
Copper silk gossamer
    ribbon

This bouquet is for those craving a more saccharine design, with sweet shades of vanilla-colored dried florals framed by frosting-pink ferns. It's perfect to give to the friend who loves all things feminine, and can easily be plunked in a vase for display (as I've done here). Most of the ingredients are bleached and/or preserved, so you'll need to source them from online stores like Afloral or go to your local florist. Due to its fluffy nature, limonium has a tendency to get tangled, so use extra care when handling it.

1. Hold the 3 stems of leather fern in one hand to form a tripod. Since these droop and bend, they will move around a bit as you add other ingredients.

2. Add 3 stems of rice flower low down between the leather ferns to help create a strong support structure.

3. Place 3 stems of limonium just above the rice flower, crisscrossing the stems so you have a fuller base.

4. Add a few stems of craspedia, concentrating them in the center and placing them at different depths throughout the bouquet.

5. Fill in the base of the bouquet with the rest of the rice flower.

6. Continue adding limonium close to the base, crisscrossing the stems.

7. Trim the winged everlasting and place them throughout the bouquet to add visual interest.

8. Place any remaining limonium and craspedia at varying depths to balance the overall look of the bouquet.

9. Trim the stems to an even length. Tie off the bouquet with the ribbon for a feminine look.

NOTE: Refer to page 30 for a step-by-step look at creating a hand-tied bouquet.

All-White Arrangement

What You'll Need

Small pedestal vase
Pin frog
Floral putty
Chicken wire
Clear cellophane floral tape
6 to 8 stems lunaria seed pods, seeds and husks removed
15 to 20 stems bleached strawflower
8 to 12 stems baby's breath

Ivory hues and easy-to-find materials make for an effortlessly chic tabletop arrangement that's perfect for a wedding or bridal shower. A few notes to guide you in the re-creation of this arrangement: Have extra baby's breath on hand, as it tends to break when you place it in the frog. To create a sense of airiness throughout, you need a strong support system to hold all of the stems upright exactly where they are placed, which is why I've called for both a tape grid and a pin frog. Finally, keep in mind that the general shape of this arrangement is triangular, with the high point at the top and the remaining ingredients gently flaring out until they are perpendicular to the vessel, forming the pyramid's base. This will help you orient the stems as you place them.

›› TURN THE PAGE TO
SEE HOW IT'S MADE

150   LASTING IMPRESSIONS

1. Secure a pin frog in the bottom of the vase with floral putty. Place a small piece of chicken wire on top of the frog, making sure it does not pop over the edge of the vessel. Create a tape grid on the top of the vase (see page 20). Trim the tallest stem of lunaria to the desired height and place it in the center left of the pin frog. This will act as the anchor stem and is the top of the pyramid you are creating here.

2. Insert 2 shorter stems of lunaria so they flank the anchor stem and add more volume around it. These will shift slightly as you add ingredients to the arrangement.

3. Continue adding shorter stems of lunaria, concentrated on the left side so that they gradually slope downward from the top of the anchor stem.

4. Trimming as you go, add 4 or 5 strawflower stems, with a concentration at the bottom. Arrange 1 or 2 stems so they hang over the edge of the vase.

5. Trim a few clusters of baby's breath and place them on the right side of the arrangement.

6. Add the remaining strawflower in the bottom center. They should splay outward so that the center looks fuller and the arrangement gets lighter toward the outer corners of the base of the pyramid. Fill any holes with the remaining baby's breath, and replace any that broke during the design process. Adjust any lunaria stems that shifted when you placed the other florals.

1

4

2

3

5

6

Plumosa and Peony Wreath

What You'll Need

12-inch (30 cm) premade grapevine base (or create your own; see page 27)
Bind wire
5 long stems bleached plumosa
7 stems purple cottage yarrow
3 peonies (1 bright pink, 2 light pink)
10 to 15 lavender hydrangea pieces
5 stems clematis
Very long off-white silk gossamer ribbon

For this design, I've used delicate ingredients like peonies and hydrangeas that seem to float on a grapevine base for an earthy, organic feel. You can forage for wild grapevine and create your own handmade wreath base in an effort to lessen your environmental impact.

1. Tightly wrap the bottom section of the wreath base with bind wire.

2. Lay out the plumosa on top of the wreath to plan which ones you'll want to lay across the base and which to drape down the front. (A little planning helps here since the length of each plumosa will be different.)

3. Attach the longest plumosa stem following the shape of the wreath base: Insert the base of each stem underneath the bind wire and gently cover the wreath base. As you move along the curve of the wreath base, tuck the top of each plumosa stem into the grapevine to secure it. Cover the rest of the wreath base with the plumosa, reserving the shorter stems for the bottom front of the wreath.

4. Trim the yarrow and insert them in the bottom center of the wreath, slipping them underneath the bind wire and into the grapevine. As you add them, the arrangement will begin to feel more secure.

5. Trim the bright pink peony and place it in the center of the focal area. This is the star of the show, so to speak, so be sure to angle it out and up. Trim the light pink peonies and place them on either side of the bright pink peony, one to the left and one angled up toward the center of the wreath.

6. Add hydrangea pieces anywhere that needs a boost of color. I concentrated them in the focal area but also added a few small pieces in the upper right of the wreath for visual interest.

7. Trim the clematis and add them around the peonies.

8. After you've placed all materials in the wreath, wrap the wreath with a bit more bind wire in any places that need additional support. The materials should look as though they are floating, so keep the wire to a minimum.

9. Tie the ribbon in a very loopy bow with long tails. Secure it to the underside of the wreath base with bind wire so it doesn't interfere with the delicate look.

NOTE: Refer to page 28 for more wreath-making guidance.

Purple Xeranthemum and Moss

What You'll Need

Large urn
Chicken wire
8 ounces (225 g) Spanish moss, plus more for the base
4 bunches purple xeranthemum
10 to 15 stems baby's breath

When it comes to dried florals, context is important—by which I mean thinking about where an arrangement will live prior to designing it. This is an often overlooked but important part of the floral design process. You'd be surprised by how differently you see an arrangement if it's not in the environment you expect. Originally inspired by a window display in a high-end women's clothing store, this arrangement straddles the line between dead and décor. If I were to put this outside, you might think it was a forgotten planter, but when I place it inside, lifted off the ground, the design becomes intentional and more elevated, both literally and figuratively.

1. Place chicken wire in the urn so it comes just above the edge. Sparsely cover the chicken wire with the moss, draping it down along the sides of the urn.

2. Select several of the tallest xeranthemum from each bunch and place a handful of them in the center of the urn. Since the final shape of the design is a dome, these will act as the anchor stems while you complete the arrangement.

3. Trimming as you go, continue to place xeranthemum to the left and right of the anchor stems to build out the domed, oval shape of the arrangement.

4. Once the overall shape has been filled out, add baby's breath low along the front and sides for additional texture.

5. To make the arrangement feel more organic, drape additional moss along the sides as needed so that it overflows.

NOTE: If you prefer a brighter look, spray the finished arrangement with a very light coat of a medium purple paint or floral spray paint that closely matches the xeranthemum. I recommend holding the can down by the base of the stems and spraying upward so you don't paint the urn. You can also drape an old towel around it to avoid accidentally painting it.

Garden-Style Bud Vases with Ranunculus

What You'll Need

7 glass bud vases of
  varying heights
10 to 15 stems light green
  cress
7 to 9 stems 'Flamingo
  Feather' celosia
20 to 25 stems
  strawflower, in various
  colors
3 stems purple ranunculus
  (see Note)
7 to 9 stems clematis

Bud vases are the perfect showcase for those delicate stems that broke during processing but that you've become emotionally attached to and can't bear to get rid of. Ranunculus is notoriously difficult to work with in its dried state; I had planned on using it in another arrangement, but I kept breaking the stems in half and realized they were better suited for this design.

The key to working with bud vases is to use an odd-numbered grouping of them in varying heights. This creates more visual interest and depth in the overall design.

1. Arrange the bud vases with the smallest in front and the tallest in back. Leave a little space between them to avoid tangling the stems and to give a light and airy feel to the overall design.

2. Trim the cress. Remove any offshoots and set them aside.

3. Trim the celosia. Place 1 or 2 small pieces each of cress (it's okay to use the offshoots) and celosia in the smaller vases and 1 or 2 longer stems of each in the taller vases.

4. Add the strawflower, placing 4 or 5 stems in the taller vases and just 1 or 2 in the smaller ones. Trim each stem to the appropriate length as you go.

5. Add 1 ranunculus each to three of the vases, placing it where a pop of color is needed. For maximum visual impact, place 1 stem in one of the front two smaller vases and the other 2 stems in the center middle and right middle taller vases.

6. Add clematis to each vase, placing 2 stems in the taller vases and 1 in the smaller ones. Trim each stem to the appropriate length as you go.

7. Take in the whole grouping, and make adjustments to any vases that look overstuffed.

NOTE: Spray roses make a great substitute if you cannot find ranunculus, which are notoriously difficult to dry.

Spanish Moss Installation

What You'll Need

Chicken wire
Zip ties
Command hooks (any type, but I recommend a smaller size so they are easily hidden)
36 ounces (1 kg) Spanish moss
20 to 25 stems white winged everlasting

Installing a site-specific piece might seem intimidating, but this one is surprisingly straightforward. You'll use a chicken wire tube for a support system that can easily be adjusted to fit the space you have to work with—this arrangement is easiest to design and install on-site. The basic design, made with Spanish moss and winged everlasting, can also be altered to include any additional florals that you have on hand, so feel free to get creative!

1. Roll a long piece of chicken wire into a tube; the overall length and diameter will depend on the chosen location. (The mantel pictured here is approximately 5 feet/1.5 m long.) Zip-tie the back of the tube together and attach it to your chosen surface with Command hooks.

2. Push large handfuls of moss through the openings in the chicken wire to secure them. Check the fullness and placement of each addition, ensuring it covers the chicken wire. The trickiest part will be untangling clumps and making the moss drape down along the front of your surface. Continue adding moss until you achieve the overall look and feel you want.

3. Trim the winged everlasting to various lengths and place them up and down the entire arrangement. Take care to angle them out in different directions to give an organic feel.

4. Once you've finished the material placement, take a step back and view the arrangement from a distance. Then make any necessary adjustments.

Soft Grass and Paper Daisies

What You'll Need

Round narrow-neck vase
5 stems light green cress
½ bunch Indian ricegrass
7 to 9 stems white
    acroclinium (paper
    daisies)
3 to 5 stems preserved
    light pink tiki fern

I find the connections between fashion and beauty and floral design endlessly fascinating. For me, this arrangement is the equivalent of French girl hair: wildly romantic, effortless, with an organic, natural feel. This project also makes a perfect bouquet—simply take it out of the vase and tie it off with a silk ribbon bow when you're ready to gift it. I recommend searching Etsy for tiki fern, but don't fret if you can't find it; needle grass makes an excellent substitute.

1. Trim the cress on the shorter side and place 3 stems in a triangular shape in the vase. They will serve as the support system for the whole arrangement.

2. Trim the ricegrass and layer it in, a few stems at a time, throughout the arrangement. (This arrangement should have a slightly wild feel, so it shouldn't be too symmetrical or tightly bunched together.)

3. Add the remaining cress in the back to help support the arrangement.

4. Trim the acroclinium and place one in the top left and one deep in the center to create a sense of depth. Add the others in a balanced but organic fashion throughout.

5. Add a few pieces of the tiki fern to the sides and back of the arrangement for additional movement.

Celosia and Indian Ricegrass Wreath

What You'll Need

10-inch (25 cm) handmade
grapevine base (see
page 27)
Bind wire
1 stem kiwi vine
3 milkweed pod branches
1 bunch Indian ricegrass
20 to 25 stems 'Flamingo
Feather' celosia
Dusty rose ribbon (at least
8 feet/2.5 m)

In contrast to the expected bulky, circular wreath design, adding branches that jut out creates a wild sense of movement and more visual interest. I recommend creating your own grapevine wreath for this design so that you can control its width, keeping it on the thinner side so it does not detract from the delicate ricegrass and celosia. Note that milkweed pod branches can be difficult to source, but you can swap in additional kiwi vine stems for a similar effect.

1. Wrap bind wire around the portion of the wreath base that will be covered by florals, leaving room for the ribbon. Tightly tie off the bind wire on the back.

2. Lay out the kiwi vine and milkweed branches to determine your preferred placement. Place the kiwi vine horizontally across the top of the wreath so it shoots out from the wreath base. Intersect the first milkweed with the kiwi vine; place the second on the bottom left, pointed outward; and set the third parallel to the left side of the wreath, pointing straight up. Once you have settled on their placement, insert them underneath the bind wire to secure them.

3. Break the Indian ricegrass into 10 smaller bunches. Insert them along the arc of the wreath base, trimming the stems as necessary so they don't stick out. Continue placing bunches around the base, leaving room to place the ribbon on the side.

4. Create bundles of 2 or 3 stems celosia each. Working your way around the wreath, insert 1 mini bundle at a time into the ricegrass, distributing them evenly.

5. Cut the ribbon into four equal pieces, each at least 24 inches (61 cm) long. Tie each in a loopy bow on the right side of the wreath, leaving the ribbon tails to lie on top of one another.

6. Since the ribbon placement adds visual weight to the wreath, step back and evaluate if you need to add any more ricegrass or celosia to balance the final design.

NOTE: Refer to page 28 for more wreath-making guidance.

Milkweed Pods and Pincushion Protea

What You'll Need

Bouquet vase or urn
Chicken wire
3 milkweed pod branches
6 to 9 stems bleached
   lunaria seed pods
5 stems pincushion protea
5 to 7 stems clematis
7 to 9 stems globe thistle
2 to 4 curly willow
   branches

Envisioned as the perfect arrangement for a formal foyer, the unusual pairing of milkweed pods and proteas is reminiscent of romantic old-world style without feeling stuffy. One way I like to elevate expectations of dried floral design is to use unexpected materials (here, that's milkweed pods) alongside more common ones (globe thistles) to create a modern aesthetic. Placing the leggy curly willow branches and milkweed pods asymmetrically gives the arrangement a sense of visual interest. Choose at least one extra-long milkweed pod branch to create a similar effect.

1. Place chicken wire in the vase, pushing it down low beneath the edge of the opening.

2. Trim the tallest milkweed branch and place it in the vase, angled to the left. This will serve as the anchor stem. Trim a second branch shorter than the first and angle it out toward the right side. Trim the third branch and place it front and center.

3. Trimming as you go, use the lunaria to fill out the shape of the arrangement, placing a tall stem in the center back and concentrating smaller pieces in the front. Lunaria stems can be quite full, so you may need to remove some smaller pieces from the stems so the arrangement does not look overstuffed.

4. Trim the protea and place one down low in front, one high in the back, and the others near the center, angled outward. Be sure they are not hidden by any other stems.

5. Trim the clematis and place them near the protea. (The cotton-ball texture of the clematis will help add softness to the arrangement without detracting from the other stems.)

6. Trim the globe thistle and place one down low, one high up, and the others deep in the center—this will help the arrangement feel lighter as your eye moves from one stem to another across it.

7. Place the curly willow branches throughout the arrangement to add movement. I've added them to the far sides, reaching both outward and toward the center.

← Embrace the dried pincushion proteas' naturally curvy stems and wiry flower heads to infuse the design with a sense of movement.

↑ Bleached lunaria with the seeds still in the pods have a polka-dot look, which adds texture and depth to the arrangement.

FESTIVE

IV.

Everlasting holiday décor used to mean glitter-covered plastic trees, but no longer. The seasonal spirit can shine year after year with these elevated dried décor options, from a sculptural cranberry-red tabletop arrangement to greenery-wrapped candlesticks and even moss mini trees. You'll want to pull these modern-feeling arrangements out every holiday season for an added dose of festive floral merriment.

Low bowl
Rectangle pin frog
Floral putty
5 preserved copper beech
   leaf branches
3 stems natural ammi
7 stems natural wheat
3 stems bupleurum

Autumnal Ammi and Wheat

A piece of design advice I received years ago is to think about how a bee would buzz around the arrangement. Would it have room to move around each element? A little breathing room is often needed, especially in seasonal dried floral designs, which can easily end up overstuffed. (For more on using negative space in your designs, see page 24.)

Keeping that philosophy in mind, this arrangement was envisioned as a piece for a minimalist who is hosting Thanksgiving and wants a table-top arrangement to suit their taste. It has all the hallmark elements of classic seasonal décor (leaves! wheat!) but has been updated in a lighter, airier design.

1. Attach the pin frog to the inside of the vessel with floral putty.

2. Trim the longest copper beech branch and insert it in the center of the arrangement, angling it out and to the left. This will be the anchor stem.

3. Trim the ammi and place them in the center front of the arrangement in a triangular shape. The longest stem should form the top of the triangle, followed by the next tallest forming the right point and the shortest forming the left point.

4. Trimming as you go, place the remaining copper beech branches on both sides of the arrangement so they splay out to the sides.

5. Trim the wheat stems and add them around the ammi.

6. Trim the bupleurum very short and add to the base of the arrangement on the right side.

Foraged Fall Leaves and Branches

What You'll Need

Large urn
Chicken wire
Floral tape
Dark orange spray paint
   (optional)
3 foraged fall branches
   with leaves attached
10 to 12 preserved copper
   beech branches
7 stems red-orange protea
5 stems dark-orange
   preserved plumosa
9 stems crocosmia pods
   with leaves attached

The red-orange and copper hues of this over-the-top design instantly make any room feel warm and cozy. A few notes on sourcing: When foraging for fall branches, look for ones that still have colorful dried leaves on them and a slight curve; this will add visual interest to the design. If you cannot find crocosmia pods, substitute a soft dried grass that will drape well. Finally, a quick online search should yield preserved, painted plumosa, but you can also get fresh stems and color them yourself with a light coat of spray paint. Be warned, though, that if you go this route, the plumosa will shed a bit as they dry out in the arrangement.

1. Fill the urn with a ball of chicken wire and secure it with 2 pieces of floral tape, crossing in the center. This will provide support for the tall branches to ensure they stay upright. Lightly paint the plumosa if desired, to help brighten the natural color and to keep it from shedding.

2. Place the tallest foraged branch in the center left of the urn. This will serve as the anchor stem. Add the remaining foraged branches to the right and left of the anchor stem.

3. Trim the copper beech branches and distribute them on the left and right sides in an organic fashion. Angle them outward so they drape and give the arrangement a sense of movement.

4. Trim the protea to varying heights and add them to the center. Place the plumosa throughout the arrangement to add texture and fill in any obvious holes. Place one stem so that it falls out and down the left side of the urn.

5. Trim the crocosmia and add them around the protea so that they shoot out and drape downward.

↑ Spray-painting dried plumosa helps keep it from shedding when you handle it or move it around in an arrangement.

→ You'll often find protea available for sale as flower heads attached to wooden stems (which sometimes loosen and fall off). Use hot glue if you need to reattach them or if you want to change the direction that they face.

Golden Eucalyptus and Strawflower Bouquet

What You'll Need

15 to 20 stems preserved yellow eucalyptus
8 to 10 stems light orange strawflower
7 to 9 stems solidago
7 to 9 stems dark red celosia
4 to 6 bupleurum
Frayed burgundy velvet ribbon

If you're like me, you find the scent of a craft store both nostalgic and comforting, thanks to the plentiful preserved eucalyptus that always seems to be in stock no matter which store you stop into. Designed as the perfect host(ess) gift for a fall event, this bouquet opens up nicely when displayed in a vase and will look right at home on the Thanksgiving table. If you can't find dried bupleurum, Queen Anne's lace is a wonderful substitute, and golden yarrow or craspedia work in place of solidago.

1. Hold 3 stems of eucalyptus in a crisscross fashion to form a tripod, including the tallest piece, which should angle out toward the center left. Add more eucalyptus stems so that they naturally splay outward in all directions.

2. Add 3 or 4 strawflower stems in the center front.

3. Insert a few more eucalyptus to support the strawflower.

4. Add 3 or 4 solidago around the strawflower.

5. Arrange the remaining strawflower stems in the center front.

6. Layer in the rest of the solidago near the strawflower to add a hint of coolness to the otherwise warm-toned bouquet.

7. Place the celosia anywhere that needs a pop of color.

8. Add the remaining eucalyptus on the sides.

9. Position the bupleurum so they jut out from the front of the bouquet.

10. Trim the stems to an even length. Tie off the bouquet with the ribbon.

NOTE: Refer to page 30 for a step-by-step look at creating a hand-tied bouquet.

Red and Green Arrangement

What You'll Need

Small pedestal vase
Pin frog
Floral putty
Chicken wire
6 to 8 stems forest green
    preserved plumosa
3 stems deep red protea
8 stems white winged
    everlasting

Creating an arrangement with a classic Christmas color combination felt like a personal design challenge that I knew I had to tackle. So often when we see dried floral décor at the holidays, it feels overstuffed and overdone and doesn't reflect our day-to-day design sensibilities. So here's an alternative made with just three ingredients. It still adds a sense of whimsy and drama to the holiday but doesn't feel like a stage prop.

1. Adhere a pin frog to the inside of the vase with floral putty. Layer a small piece of chicken wire on top of it for added stability.

2. Trim a medium-length plumosa stem and place it in the center right of the vase. Place the longest stem of plumosa on the right side so it spills outward. Trim another medium-length plumosa and add it to the center left.

3. Since the protea are the focal point of the arrangement, take your time to place each with care. Think about the whole form of the arrangement, taking a moment to step back and view it from different angles after you place each one. To begin, take the tallest protea, trim it, and place it at the center back of the arrangement, angling it slightly outward.

4. Trim the second-tallest protea and place it in the center left of the vase. Trim the last protea stem to the shortest length and insert it in the base so that it sits upright and is angled out and over the edge of the vessel. The three protea should form a loose triangle.

5. Add the remaining plumosa to form a domed shape when viewed from the front. Take care to add the shorter stems in front to help cover the chicken wire.

6. Trim the winged everlasting to varying heights and distribute them throughout the arrangement.

PLUMOSA

I gravitate toward plumosa for holiday-themed projects, as it naturally imitates the greenery we see all season long. Preserved plumosa is preferable to naturally dried because it doesn't shed and retains its flexibility. However, if you want to prioritize sustainability, naturally dried plumosa will work, too; you'll just need to keep an eye out for fallen bits after using it in your designs.

When treated as the main ingredient in a wreath or tabletop arrangement, plumosa immediately makes a space feel festive. We often see dead, lifeless botanicals during the winter months; I use plumosa in holiday designs as a contrast, because each stem has an inherent sense of movement and life that is so difficult to find then. And because it keeps for ages, you can pull it out year after year, and it will still look like new.

Source plumosa at specialty online retailers or your local floral shop or wholesaler. You may also find it under its common name, asparagus fern.

Cranberry Celosia

What You'll Need

Large pedestal vase
Pin frog
Floral putty
Chicken wire
Floral tape
40 to 45 stems red celosia
Toothpicks

This arrangement may be time-consuming, but don't let that deter you. The time it takes to perfect the triangular, trefoil-type shape will absolutely be worth it. And you can display this showstopper year after year—since it uses just one material in a more traditional arrangement, the risk of its going out of style is quite low. I recommend using a metallic gold pedestal vase as the base for a classic, Christmasy color combination.

›› TURN THE PAGE TO
SEE HOW IT'S MADE

1. Adhere a pin frog to the inside of the vase with floral putty. For additional support, cover the frog with chicken wire so it comes up just over the edge of the vessel. Since you are using a vase with a wide mouth, you'll need additional support to keep the chicken wire in place; tape a single-square grid on top. Identify the largest pieces of celosia, the ones with smallish flower heads and long stems, and the ones with the smallest flower heads. Set the smallest ones aside.

2. Begin building the bottom portion of the arrangement with the larger, bulkier celosia. Trim one and add it to the left side so that it hangs over the edge of the vase.

3. Find the bulkiest, tallest piece of celosia and place it directly in the middle of the chicken wire, making sure it securely attaches to the pin frog at the bottom. These two stem placements will help guide you as you build out the rest of the piece.

4. Continue adding large celosia around the circumference of the vase, establishing the circular outside of the arrangement.

5. Trim and begin adding the longer celosia with smaller heads on top of the bulkier pieces. Press the stems down into the frog so they stay in place. As you build upward, frequently take a step back to ensure you are creating a triangular shape. It should be widest at the bottom and gradually get smaller as you move upward. As the arrangement grows, use toothpicks to secure pieces to one another if they need a little more support.

6. Use the reserved small stems to fill in any holes and insert a final small piece on top to create a trefoil shape. After you've moved the arrangement to where you'll be displaying it, gently adjust any pieces that have shifted.

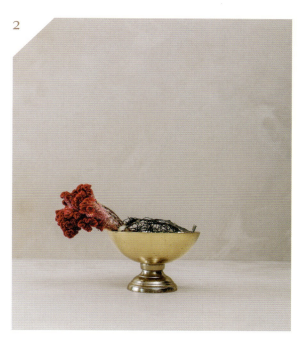

2

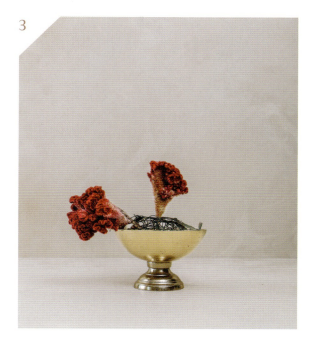

3

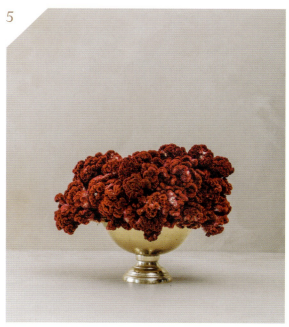

5

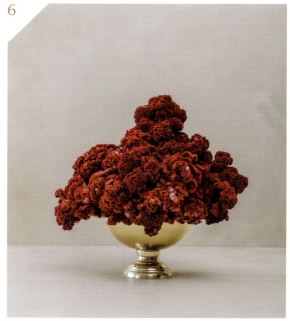

6

2 tall candlesticks
Chicken wire
Zip ties
10 stems preserved
    hedera
5 stems sabulosum cones

Greenery-Wrapped Candlesticks

Dressing up candlesticks with dried and preserved botanicals has become one of my favorite ways to add more flowers to a table. If you cannot source hedera, eucalyptus is a great substitute. And though this design is meant for the holiday season, you can use the same technique with other leafy stems that would be appropriate any time of year—just be sure they are flexible in their dried or preserved state. For a coquette-style aesthetic, add a few layered bows to the top of the greenery.

1. Cover the base and sides of the candlesticks tightly with chicken wire. Secure the chicken wire with zip ties, taking care to fold in the jagged ends of the chicken wire so they don't stick out. Trim the ends of the zip ties.

2. Trim off groupings of hedera leaves and insert the stems into the chicken wire until both candlesticks are covered, with the bottom of each candlestick a bit fuller than the top.

3. Trim off smaller pieces of the sabulosum and insert them into the chicken wire, with some deeper into the chicken wire and others popping out.

4. Take note of how the candlesticks look next to each other, making sure they are roughly the same overall size, and make adjustments if necessary.

NOTE: Please don't leave candles unattended while they are burning!

Moss Mini Trees

What You'll Need

2 craft foam cones: one
  18 by 4¾ inches
  (46 by 12 cm), one
  12 by 4 inches (30.5 by
  10 cm)
About 8 ounces (225 g)
  preserved Spanish moss
Floral pins
Black velvet ribbon
  (optional)
Battery-operated warm
  white LED fairy lights
  (at least 10 feet/3 m;
  optional)

Technically, these are topiaries, but I'm calling them mini trees because anything that comes in a mini version is immediately cuter than the original. (I don't make the rules!) Is this a craft project? Maybe. There have been times over the years that floral design has surprised me and landed me in a craft store looking for a niche tool or material. I've learned to not get too hung up on labels—no matter what we design or create, it's artistic expression. I've used Spanish moss here, for a drapey effect, but most kinds of preserved moss will work in this design. If you'd like to avoid craft foam in favor of a more sustainable approach, reuse a block of packing foam or form a cone with cardboard.

1. Cover each cone entirely with handfuls of moss. Secure the moss with floral pins.

2. You can leave the trees unadorned, or tie a large ribbon bow so the tails will drape down the front of one tree and secure it at the top with a floral pin.

Alternatively, attach small bows all over a tree for a feminine look, or wrap with fairy lights for added holiday cheer.

NOTE: The exact amount of moss necessary to cover each cone can vary, so it's best to overbuy.

Sculptural Holiday Wreath with Plumosa

What You'll Need

12-inch (30 cm) handmade
    grapevine wreath base
    (see page 27)
Chicken wire
Zip ties
3 curvy foraged grapevines
10 stems preserved
    plumosa
4 stems tallow berry
3 stems sabulosum cones
Hot glue gun
Cranberry velvet ribbon
Bind wire

Once the temperatures start to drop and the leaves have fallen from the trees, consider going foraging for grapevine to use for a wreath. You can find wild grapevine in many different habitats. It tends to grow in long-sweeping, curved shapes, making it perfect for this design—sourcing vines with a bend is critical to the success of this arrangement. Simply set them aside and let them dry out on their own. If they dry in a shape you don't like, you can reshape them by soaking them in water and bending them into the desired form. Use a zip tie or twine to hold the shape as the vines dry out again. If you cannot find sabulosum, substitute small pinecones.

›› TURN THE PAGE TO
    SEE HOW IT'S MADE

1. Wrap a section of chicken wire around the lower left portion of the wreath base so there is a little room to put stems into it. Secure it on the back with 2 zip ties. Cut off the tails of the zip ties.

2. Add 1 foraged vine so it intersects the left side of the wreath base. Insert one end into the chicken wire and the other end through the base so it bisects the base. Add 2 plumosa, one that goes around the left side of the base and drapes downward and one draped at the top. Tuck the stems into the base. Trim the longest stem of tallow berry and add it to the bottom of the wreath so it sticks out toward the right side.

3. Trim the remaining vines. Add one to the far left side of the wreath and the other along the top, taking care to work with the natural curve of each. (Yours may look slightly different from the example, and that's okay; you want a feel of organic movement with each placement.) Secure the vines with bind wire if necessary. (This will help inform the placement of the rest of the tallow berry so it feels organic.) Add plumosa stems with the pieces draping off the base so the wreath looks organically shaped. Add another stem of tallow berry to help balance the added plumosa.

4. Add the remaining plumosa around the entire piece and adjust so that the placement feels balanced. You should be able to see the wreath base through the plumosa in places.

5. Place the rest of the tallow berry stems and the sabulosum around the wreath. Concentrate the tallow berry at the bottom left; evenly distribute the sabulosum. Play around with the placement of each until it is to your liking. Hot-glue the tallow berry and sabulosum stems to the wreath.

6. Tie the ribbon into a loopy bow and attach it to the lower right section of the wreath with bind wire.

1

4

2

3

5

6

20 to 25 stems woolly
betony
16 to 20 stems white
tallow berry
Frayed cream velvet ribbon

White Tallow Berry and Woolly Betony Bouquet

A design strategy I often employ is to err on the side of simplicity. That can mean using fewer ingredients than I might otherwise or removing more flower heads and leaves from a stem to eliminate bulk and prevent an arrangement from feeling like it has too much going on. Here, with just two ingredients I've created a bouquet that lets each one shine and still has an old-world holiday feel. To replicate this look, thoroughly process the woolly betony and white tallow berry, removing secondary stems and leaves to allow the berries and blooms at the top stand out.

1. Use 3 stems of woolly betony to create the tripod base support structure.

2. Continue adding woolly betony, crisscrossing the stems until you achieve a nice, fluffy base.

3. Add the first few tallow berry stems, concentrating on the center and placing them at different depths throughout the bouquet.

4. Trim another 5 to 7 tallow berry stems and add them in a crisscross fashion for more support, sinking each one down toward the base to create additional depth.

5. Add any remaining woolly betony next to the tallow berry to create a sense of fullness.

6. Place each of the remaining tallow berry stems at varying heights so that they are evenly dispersed throughout the bouquet.

7. Trim the stems to an even length. Tie off the bouquet with the ribbon.

NOTE: Refer to page 30 for a step-by-step look at creating a hand-tied bouquet.

Dried Citrus, Plumosa, and Branches

What You'll Need

Medium jug
Chicken wire
5 lichen-covered branches
8 to 10 stems preserved
    bleached plumosa
Fishing line
5 stems tallow berry
10 dried orange slices

Displaying sculptural branches as home décor has developed into a trend you've likely seen from your favorite interior designer or influencer over the past few years. No matter the branches' state, relying on their inherent dramatic quality always makes them a showstopper.

Here is a shockingly easy-to-make winter branch arrangement with a few additional materials to play up the frosty color palette—dried oranges are added for a more festive look. You can purchase dried orange slices or make them yourself (see page 33 for instructions). If you can't source lichen-covered branches, you can create them yourself by hot-gluing reindeer moss to foraged branches; you can find preserved bleached plumosa on Etsy and Afloral.

1. Insert a small piece of chicken wire into the jug.

2. Place the branches in the jug. Angle the tallest one outward to the left and arrange the others so they are splayed out.

3. Layer plumosa on top of the branches and loosely wrap it around each branch, one by one. Insert the smaller pieces of plumosa at the edge of the jug.

4. Trim the tallow berry stems to varying heights and place them throughout the base of the arrangement. Take care to place the shortest piece in front and angle it so that it spills over the rim of the vase.

5. Attach fishing line to the orange slices and tie off each length, creating a little hoop so they will hang on the branches. Hook each one onto a branch until you achieve an even distribution throughout the arrangement.

↓ Delicate tallow berries complement the wintry color palette here and help fill any holes in the base of the design.

→ You may want to dry more orange slices than called for so that you can choose the best-looking ones to display front and center in this unexpected yet festive arrangement. Any extras can be used for decorating a Christmas tree or as tabletop décor.

Library of Ingredients

This list is a brief collection of dried botanicals that I find myself gravitating toward over and over again. It is by no means exhaustive but should help when sourcing materials or looking for more information on a single ingredient.

1. Amaranthus

SCIENTIFIC NAME: *Amaranthus caudatus*
OTHER COMMON NAME: Love-lies-bleeding
PREFERRED DRYING METHOD: Air-dry
FEATURED ON PAGES 41, 46, 51, 53, 62, 67, 77

There are two prevalent varieties of amaranthus: hanging (pictured at left) and upright (at right). Both types hold their color well when preserved and add dramatic movement to designs. They can be found mostly at floral wholesalers.

2. Ammi

SCIENTIFIC NAME: *Ammi visnaga*
OTHER COMMON NAMES: Toothpick weed; bishop's weed
PREFERRED DRYING METHOD: Hang-dry
FEATURED ON PAGES 98, 174

These hearty seed heads can be used as large focal points in arrangements. Look for them at craft and hobby stores.

3. Baby's Breath

SCIENTIFIC NAME: *Gypsophila paniculata*
OTHER COMMON NAME: Gyp
PREFERRED DRYING METHODS: Evaporation or air-dry
FEATURED ON PAGES 108, 150, 156

Easy to dry at home, baby's breath absorbs spray paint readily. It works in a number of design styles.

4. Banksia

SCIENTIFIC NAME: *Banksia serrata*
PREFERRED DRYING METHOD: Air-dry
FEATURED ON PAGE 111

A type of protea, this Australian native plant adds a bold, dramatic design element anywhere you use it. It is available at many online retailers.

5. Bracken Fern

SCIENTIFIC NAME: *Pteridium aquilinum*
OTHER COMMON NAMES: Brack; bracken; eagle fern
PREFERRED DRYING METHOD: Air-dry
FEATURED ON PAGES 98, 130

This common fern is great for autumnal designs and can be painted to fit any aesthetic. Try foraging for this material, as it grows wild in many areas.

6. Bunny Tails

SCIENTIFIC NAME: *Lagurus ovatus*
PREFERRED DRYING METHOD: Hang-dry
FEATURED ON PAGE 77

These cute, fluffy tufts add whimsy to designs. If you want to color them, they are better suited to dyeing (as shown here) than spray-painting.

7. Bupleurum

SCIENTIFIC NAME: *Bupleurum falcatum*
OTHER COMMON NAMES: Sickle-leaved hare's ear; thorow wax
PREFERRED DRYING METHOD: Air-dry
FEATURED ON PAGES 174, 180

This herb is primarily used for medicinal purposes, but it dries to reveal a delicate, wispy flower head. Look for it online at specialty floral sites or at your local wholesaler.

8. Carlina Moon Flower

SCIENTIFIC NAME: *Carlina acaulis*
OTHER COMMON NAMES: Silver, dwarf carline, and stemless carline thistle
PREFERRED DRYING METHODS: Air-dry, hang-dry
FEATURED ON PAGE 65

Handle these silvery beauties with caution, as the spiny stems have sharp points. The stems are short, making them ideal for detail work on wreaths or small installations. Look for them at specialty floral shops and flower farms.

9. Cecropia Leaf

SCIENTIFIC NAME: *Cecropia peltata*
PREFERRED DRYING METHOD: Air-dry
FEATURED ON PAGE 46

A sculptural statement maker, cecropia leaf is pretty enough to display on its own. It can be hard to find, though, so contact your local wholesaler or floral shop to help you source it.

10. Celosia

SCIENTIFIC NAMES: *Celosia cristata*; *C. argentea*
OTHER COMMON NAME: Silver cockscomb
PREFERRED DRYING METHOD: Air-dry
FEATURED ON PAGES 159, 165, 180, 187

Available in a number of different varieties (pictured here: crested cockscomb, left, and 'Flamingo Feather'), celosia adds color and visual interest to any arrangement.

11. Clematis

SCIENTIFIC NAME: *Clematis vitalba*
OTHER COMMON NAME: Old man's beard
PREFERRED DRYING METHOD: Air-dry
FEATURED ON PAGES 82, 103, 155, 159, 166

These sweet cotton-ball puffs impart a touch of whimsy and softness to arrangements and wreaths. Try foraging for clematis, as it grows wild in many areas.

12. Copper Beech

SCIENTIFIC NAME: *Fagus sylvatica*
PREFERRED DRYING METHOD: Hang-dry
FEATURED ON PAGES 174, 177

Copper beech is widely available from online retailers in preserved varieties in shades of brown, red, and orange, making it ideal for autumnal designs.

LIBRARY OF INGREDIENTS

13. Craspedia

SCIENTIFIC NAME: *Craspedia globosa*
OTHER COMMON NAMES: Billy balls; billy buttons
PREFERRED DRYING METHOD: Air-dry
FEATURED ON PAGES 58, 149

These mustard-yellow flower heads are incredibly easy to dry at home, and can often be found at craft outlets or grocery stores that carry flowers. They are great for painting and can also be bleached (shown opposite, right).

14. Cress

SCIENTIFIC NAME: *Lepidium sativum*
OTHER COMMON NAME: Ornamental cress
PREFERRED DRYING METHOD: Hang-dry
FEATURED ON PAGES 77, 92, 159, 162

Cress's sturdy stems hold up well in a variety of designs. Handle them delicately, however, as they tangle easily.

15. Curly Willow

SCIENTIFIC NAME: *Salix matsudana*
OTHER COMMON NAMES: Corkscrew willow; twisted willow
PREFERRED DRYING METHOD: Air-dry
FEATURED ON PAGES 41, 86, 103, 121, 166

Curly willow adds a sense of movement to arrangements; it can easily be sourced online.

16. Dahlia

SCIENTIFIC NAME: *Dahlia* spp.
PREFERRED DRYING METHOD: Evaporation
FEATURED ON PAGES 45, 121

Although extremely delicate, these dried blooms retain their color quite beautifully. Look for the smaller varieties, such as *Dahlia pinnata*, from your local flower farm or shop, as they are easier to dry.

17. Delphinium

SCIENTIFIC NAME: *Delphinium elatum*
PREFERRED DRYING METHOD: Hang-dry
FEATURED ON PAGE 135

These colorful stems add height to arrangements and are great for traditional wreaths. Try to source them locally; they are grown by many small flower farms.

18. Dried Fruit

PREFERRED DRYING METHODS: Oven-dry, air-dry
FEATURED ON PAGES 53, 201

Dried sliced citrus is great for festive holiday decorations. See page 33 for instructions for oven-drying; whole fruits, like oranges and pomegranates, can also be air-dried.

19. Eucalyptus

SCIENTIFIC NAME: *Eucalyptus* spp.
PREFERRED DRYING METHOD: Hang-dry
FEATURED ON PAGES 45, 180

A craft store staple, eucalyptus is available preserved in many varieties (pictured here: 'Baby Blue'). It retains its strong scent and will add bulk to any arrangement.

20. Foxtail Millet Grass

SCIENTIFIC NAME: *Alopecurus* spp.
OTHER COMMON NAMES: Mini foxtails, millet grass
PREFERRED DRYING METHOD: Hang-dry
FEATURED ON PAGES 67, 88, 129

This beautiful, soft grass imparts a sense of calm. Look for this online from specialty retailers. Keep it away from pets, as it is toxic to animals.

21. Globe Thistle

SCIENTIFIC NAME: *Echinops* spp.
PREFERRED DRYING METHOD: Air-dry
FEATURED ON PAGES 121, 129, 166

Prickly globe thistle is easily sourced from retailers and makes a great filler stem in bouquets.

22. Gomphrena

SCIENTIFIC NAME: *Gomphrena globosa*
OTHER COMMON NAME: Globe amaranth
PREFERRED DRYING METHOD: Hang-dry
FEATURED ON PAGES 58, 126

Gomphrena is available in a wide range of colors and retains its vibrancy when dried. It looks especially impactful when used en masse in bouquets and wreaths. Find it at specialty retailers online.

23. Helichrysum

SCIENTIFIC NAME: *Helichrysum* spp.
OTHER COMMON NAMES: Curry plant; everlasting; immortelle
PREFERRED DRYING METHOD: Hang-dry
FEATURED ON PAGE 140

There are multiple varieties of helichrysum, including the two bleached varieties shown here: *H. vestitum* (left) and *H. italicum*, also known as immortelle (right). They are widely available and a great choice for bouquets.

24. Horsetail Grass

SCIENTIFIC NAME: *Nassella* (or *Stipa*) *tenuissima*
OTHER COMMON NAME: Mexican feather grass
PREFERRED DRYING METHOD: Air-dry
FEATURED ON PAGES 86, 103

This ornamental grass has a shimmering look when dried. Use it in all types of designs, from bouquets to installations.

25. Hydrangea

SCIENTIFIC NAME: *Hydrangea macrophylla*
PREFERRED DRYING METHOD: Evaporation
FEATURED ON PAGES 54, 118, 155

Available in a few different varieties, these bulbous stems are particularly well suited to installation pieces and sculptural tabletop arrangements. Buy them fresh (they are widely available) and dry them yourself.

26. Indian Ricegrass

SCIENTIFIC NAME: *Eriocoma hymenoides*
OTHER COMMON NAMES: Indian millet; sand grass
PREFERRED DRYING METHOD: Air-dry
FEATURED ON PAGES 88, 92, 118, 162, 165

This grass lends an ethereal quality to arrangements. A little goes a long way, as each stem has fluffy pieces that puff outward.

27. Kiwi Vine

SCIENTIFIC NAME: *Actinidia arguta*
OTHER COMMON NAMES: Hardy kiwi; tara vine
PREFERRED DRYING METHOD: Air-dry
FEATURED ON PAGES 75, 165

Naturally dramatic, this curvy-stemmed plant adds a sculptural quality to arrangements and wreaths.

28. Lavender

SCIENTIFIC NAME: *Lavandula* spp.
PREFERRED DRYING METHOD: Hang-dry
FEATURED ON PAGE 67

An old-world flower that's beloved everywhere, lavender retains a scent that makes it well worth using in bouquets and as a filler in arrangements.

29. Leather Fern

SCIENTIFIC NAME: *Rumohra adiantiformis*
OTHER COMMON NAME: Leatherleaf fern
PREFERRED DRYING METHOD: Air-dry
FEATURED ON PAGE 149

Look for leather fern in its preserved state from online retailers; it retains its flexibility and shape.

30. Leucadendron

SCIENTIFIC NAME: *Leucadendron salignum*
OTHER COMMON NAME: Sunshine conebush
PREFERRED DRYING METHOD: Air-dry
FEATURED ON PAGE 111

This tropical stem makes a striking focal flower in arrangements, and can be found online from specialty retailers.

31. Limonium

SCIENTIFIC NAME: *Limonium* spp.
OTHER COMMON NAMES: Sea lavender; caspia
PREFERRED DRYING METHOD: Air-dry
FEATURED ON PAGES 42, 121, 149

An affordable and easy-to-find flower, limonium is a great fluffy filler in arrangements.

32. Lotus Seed Pods

SCIENTIFIC NAME: *Nelumbo nucifera*
PREFERRED DRYING METHOD: Hang-dry
FEATURED ON PAGES 58, 67

These seed pods are widely commercially available already dried and look right at home in boho-style bouquets and arrangements.

33. Lunaria

SCIENTIFIC NAME: *Lunaria annua*
OTHER COMMON NAMES: Honesty; money plant
PREFERRED DRYING METHOD: Hang-dry
FEATURED ON PAGES 140, 150, 166

The papery thin, delicate seed pods of lunaria make for a romantic addition to arrangements. Try foraging for these in fall or purchasing them from a specialty floral retailer. You can often source them without the seeds and husks attached.

34. Miscanthus

SCIENTIFIC NAME: *Miscanthus sinensis*
PREFERRED DRYING METHOD: Air-dry
FEATURED ON PAGES 58, 75, 98, 129

Sometimes incorrectly referred to as pampas, this grass grows in the wild in many places and can be foraged, already dried, in fall.

35. Nigella

SCIENTIFIC NAME: *Nigella damascena*
OTHER COMMON NAME: Love-in-a-mist
PREFERRED DRYING METHOD: Hang-dry
FEATURED ON PAGE 124

These seed pods retain their oval shape and purple/green color well, making them an excellent choice as a secondary stem to fill out an arrangement or bouquet. They are commonly found at local flower shops.

36. Palms

SCIENTIFIC NAME: *Palmae* (family)
PREFERRED DRYING METHOD: Air-dry
FEATURED ON PAGES 41, 54, 111, 129

Palm fans and fronds come in many varieties, such as sago, tsunami, and fan palms. All can be painted, cut into specific shapes, or used without alteration for a bold design statement, like the Mexican palm fan seen here. Find them online at many specialty retailers.

37. Peony

SCIENTIFIC NAME: *Paeonia* spp.

PREFERRED DRYING METHOD: Evaporation

FEATURED ON PAGES 42, 155

This crowd favorite retains its sweet fragrance when dried, along with its charm. Be warned, though: It is extremely delicate, so I recommend that you buy fresh stems and dry them yourself.

38. Plumosa

SCIENTIFIC NAME: *Asparagus plumosus*

OTHER COMMON NAMES: Asparagus fern; lace fern

PREFERRED DRYING METHOD: Air-dry

FEATURED ON PAGES 155, 177, 182, 184, 194, 201

Preserved plumosa does not shed and retains its flexibility, making it perfect for wispy, romantic designs. It's available at many specialty online retailers.

39. Protea

SCIENTIFIC NAME: *Protea repens*

OTHER COMMON NAMES: Honey pot; sugarbush

PREFERRED DRYING METHOD: Air-dry

FEATURED ON PAGES 177, 182

These plasticky-looking flower heads become wiry and wild when dried, but the stems remain strong enough to feature in wreaths and bouquets. Reach out to a local florist or wholesaler to help you locate them.

40. Reindeer Moss

SCIENTIFIC NAME: *Cladonia rangiferina*

OTHER COMMON NAMES: Reindeer lichen; deer moss

PREFERRED DRYING METHOD: Air-dry

FEATURED ON PAGES 61, 67

Easily found at a local garden shop or craft store, this shrubby-looking greenery is great for covering mechanics or displaying in a wreath.

41. Rice Flower

SCIENTIFIC NAME: *Ozothamnus diosmifolius*

OTHER COMMON NAME: Pill flower

PREFERRED DRYING METHOD: Hang-dry

FEATURED ON PAGES 42, 149

Available in multiple colors, both bleached and preserved, these stems with dense flower heads work especially well in bouquets.

42. Rose

SCIENTIFIC NAME: *Rosa* spp.

PREFERRED DRYING METHOD: Hang-dry

FEATURED ON PAGES 42, 124

These classic flowers can be finicky in their dried form because the petals are so delicate. You can mitigate this by hanging them to dry immediately after picking or purchasing. Miniature spray roses are easier to work with, as they retain their sturdy nature.

43. Rudbeckia

SCIENTIFIC NAME: *Rudbeckia* spp.

OTHER COMMON NAMES: Coneflower; black-eyed Susan

PREFERRED DRYING METHOD: Hang-dry

FEATURED ON PAGE 129

These delicate stems retain their bright color, but because of their brittleness I recommend using only a few stems in smaller designs. Rudbeckia can be found at specialty online floral suppliers.

44. Scabiosa Pods

SCIENTIFIC NAME: *Scabiosa* spp.

PREFERRED DRYING METHOD: Air-dry

FEATURED ON PAGES 77, 97

Single stems of these pods are available at local floral shops and are great for simple ikebana-inspired designs.

45. Silver Brunia

SCIENTIFIC NAME: *Brunia albiflora*

PREFERRED DRYING METHOD: Air-dry

FEATURED ON PAGE 129

These silvery-gray stems work well as a heart, filler flower in winter arrangements. Find them at your local floral shop or online.

46. Solidago

SCIENTIFIC NAME: *Solidago* spp.

OTHER COMMON NAME: Goldenrod

PREFERRED DRYING METHOD: Hang-dry

FEATURED ON PAGES 126, 180

Stems with brightly colored, fluffy flower heads are a colorful addition to bouquets, wreaths, or detail work.

47. Spanish Moss

SCIENTIFIC NAME: *Tillandsia usneoides*

PREFERRED DRYING METHOD: Air-dry

FEATURED ON PAGES 65, 156, 160, 193

This tropical flowerless air plant adds texture and movement to any dried floral design. Look for it at your local craft store.

48. Statice

SCIENTIFIC NAME: *Limonium sinuatum*

PREFERRED DRYING METHOD: Air-dry

FEATURED ON PAGES 46, 115, 116, 121, 124

Technically this is another variety of limonium (see page 210), but this particular variety retains its bright color, works beautifully as a colorful filler in arrangements, and is widely available at retailers.

49. Strawflower

SCIENTIFIC NAME: Asteraceae (family)
OTHER COMMON NAME: Everlasting
PREFERRED DRYING METHOD: Hang-dry
FEATURED ON PAGES 58, 121, 143, 146, 150, 159, 180

You'll likely gravitate toward this easy-to-work-with and commonly available material for its versatility and variety of colors.

50. Strelitzia

SCIENTIFIC NAME: *Strelitzia* spp.
OTHER COMMON NAME: Bird of paradise
PREFERRED DRYING METHOD: Air-dry
FEATURED ON PAGES 58, 67, 111

This uniquely shaped tropical dried flower is great for spray-painting and use in uniquely shaped arrangements. Source it online from specialty shops.

51. Tallow Berry

SCIENTIFIC NAME: *Triadica sebifera*
PREFERRED DRYING METHOD: Air-dry
FEATURED ON PAGES 194, 198, 201

Perfect for holiday designs, these delicate stems of clustered berries work well in bouquets and detail work for wreaths.

52. Thistle

SCIENTIFIC NAME: *Eryngium* spp.
OTHER COMMON NAME: Sea holly
PREFERRED DRYING METHODS: Air-dry, hang-dry
FEATURED ON PAGE 121

Easy to source and dry yourself, these periwinkle-blue stems retain their color during the drying process. *Eryngium planum* is pictured here, but many types of *Eryngium* are similar in appearance; all are ideal for vase arrangements or bouquet designs.

53. Wheat

SCIENTIFIC NAME: *Triticum aestivum*
PREFERRED DRYING METHODS: Air-dry, hang-dry
FEATURED ON PAGE 174

Easy to source from online retailers, these stems lend themselves to a traditional aesthetic.

54. Winged Everlasting

SCIENTIFIC NAME: *Ammobium alatum*
PREFERRED DRYING METHOD: Hang-dry
FEATURED ON PAGES 126, 149, 160, 182

These aptly named spindly stems hold up surprisingly well once dried and impart a romantic element to bouquets and tabletop arrangements. An online search will yield multiple results for retailers who sell them.

55. Woolly Betony

SCIENTIFIC NAME: *Stachys byzantina*
OTHER COMMON NAME: Lamb's ear
PREFERRED DRYING METHOD: Hang-dry
FEATURED ON PAGE 198

These soft stems impart a dreamy quality to bouquets. But be forewarned, they do break easily, so handle with care. Find at flower shops, either local or online.

56. Xeranthemum

SCIENTIFIC NAME: *Xeranthemum* spp.
PREFERRED DRYING METHOD: Hang-dry
FEATURED ON PAGES 140, 156

Add a sense of whimsy and movement to your design work with these stems. Look for them from specialty online retailers.

57. Yarrow

SCIENTIFIC NAME: *Achillea* spp.
PREFERRED DRYING METHOD: Air-dry
FEATURED ON PAGES 124, 130, 155

Available in a number of varieties at retailers, this traditional dried floral is a great go-to for bouquets, as it can act as both focal stem and filler.

Resources

Below are my favorite sources for dried and preserved florals, supplies, and tools. Additionally, check your local hardware and garden shops for tools and vessels. Your preferred large online retailer or big-box store will also likely carry support structures, supplies, and tools. And check vintage and antique shops to source unique vessels.

Abraflora
ABRAFLORA.COM
A wholesaler with an extensive inventory of dried and preserved flowers, grasses, and branches

Afloral
AFLORAL.COM
A great standby for more common dried florals; many vases and vessels for sale

Bloomist
BLOOMIST.COM
A small collection of harder-to-find dried and preserved flowers and grasses, along with floral tools and a great selection of vases and vessels

Charles Little & Company
CHARLESLITTLEANDCOMPANY.COM
High-quality dried flowers, available in monthly releases

Etsy
ETSY.COM
A plethora of sellers offering many dried floral options

The Floral Society
THEFLORALSOCIETY.COM
A well-curated assortment of modern vases, high-end tools, and other wares for the home

Gardenheir
GARDENHEIR.COM
First-rate snips, shears, and scissors sold by garden enthusiasts

Roxanne's Dried Flowers
ROXANNESDRIEDFLOWERS.COM
A woman-owned small business that offers a wide selection of dried and preserved botanicals

Saint Maide
SAINTMAIDE.COM
My dried floral studio, where I occasionally sell bundles of dried flowers in limited quantities

Terrain
SHOPTERRAIN.COM
An inspiring garden and outdoor retailer with a wide range of offerings, from preserved botanicals to large urns and vases

Tono and Co.
TONOANDCO.COM
A hand-dyed silk textile company offering ribbons in a variety of colors and finishes

Velvet Curation Co.
VELVETCURATIONCO.COM
A great selection of dried grasses and foliage

Acknowledgments

The process of writing this book has contained all of the elements of a proper story: high highs and low lows, frustrations, grateful moments, tears, and laughter. This journey has been one of the most authentic human experiences I've lived. It has been a true gift to take the time to write and create this with the intention of sharing it with all of you.

Thank you to the following people who have helped me write this book—something I always wanted to do but never thought I would. It would not have been possible without your support.

To my editor, Bridget, thank you for seeing my potential. And to the rest of the Artisan team—Lia, Laura, Nina, Suet, Donna, Annie, Julia, Zach, Moira, Theresa, and Cindy—for all of your hard work.

To Patrick, thank you for your support since before day one. I wouldn't have taken the steps to get here had you not encouraged me along the way.

To Kate, thank you for your keen photographer's eye and ongoing support.

To Kylie, the real MVP of this entire project, thank you.

To Anna, thank you for allowing us to shoot in your beautifully designed space, Stayframe.

To Caitlin, thank you for sharing your art so freely for this project.

To Bruce, thank you for the laughs and the sourcing help, but mainly the laughs.

To Winnie, thank you for the reminders to get outside, silent encouragement, and cuddles.

To Brandon, there simply would not be a book without your ongoing support and gentle encouragement. Thank you.

And finally, thank you to all you readers. I feel lucky to have so many people interested in the beautiful world of dried florals.

Index

Page numbers in *italics* indicate photographs.